A Case of Neglect?

Children's Experiences and the Sociology of Childhood

Edited by
Ian Butler and Ian Shaw

First published in 1996
by Ashgate Publishing Ltd

This edition first published in 2018 by Routledge
2 Park Square, Milton Park, Abingdon, Oxon, OX14 4RN
and by Routledge
711 Third Avenue, New York, NY 10017

Routledge is an imprint of the Taylor & Francis Group, an informa business

© 1996 I. Butler and I. Shaw

All rights reserved. No part of this book may be reprinted or reproduced or utilised in
any form or by any electronic, mechanical, or other means, now known or hereafter
invented, including photocopying and recording, or in any information storage or
retrieval system, without permission in writing from the publishers.

Publisher's Note
The publisher has gone to great lengths to ensure the quality of this reprint but points
out that some imperfections in the original copies may be apparent.

Disclaimer
The publisher has made every effort to trace copyright holders and welcomes
correspondence from those they have been unable to contact.

A Library of Congress record exists under LCCN: 96083222

ISBN 13: 978-0-8153-4783-5 (hbk)
ISBN 13: 978-1-351-16868-7 (ebk)
ISBN 13: 978-0-8153-4785-9 (pbk)

A Case of Neglect?

Children's experiences and the sociology of childhood

Edited by
IAN BUTLER
IAN SHAW

Avebury

Aldershot • Brookfield USA • Hong Kong • Singapore • Sydney

© I. Butler and I. Shaw 1996

All rights reserved. No part of this publication may be reproduced, stored in a retrieval system, or transmitted in any form or by any means, electronic, mechanical, photocopying, recording or otherwise without the prior permission of the publisher.

Published by
Avebury
Ashgate Publishing Limited
Gower House
Croft Road
Aldershot
Hants GU11 3HR
England

Ashgate Publishing Company
Old Post Road
Brookfield
Vermont 05036
USA

British Library Cataloguing in Publication Data

A case of neglect? : children's experiences and the sociology of childhood. - (Cardiff papers in qualitative research)
1. Children 2. Children - Conduct of life 3. Socialization
I. Butler, Ian,1955 - II. Shaw, Ian
305.2'3

ISBN 1 85972 048 X

Library of Congress Catalog Card Number: 96-83222

Printed and bound by Athenaeum Press, Ltd.,
Gateshead, Tyne & Wear.

Contents

List of figures and tables	vii
Notes on contributors	viii
Acknowledgements	xi

1. Children and the sociology of childhood
   Ian Butler — 1

2. Unbroken voices: Children, young people and
   qualitative methods
   Ian Shaw — 19

3. 'Mirror, mirror on the wall. Who is the fairest
   of them all?' Involuntary childlessness and identity
   Julie Selwyn — 37

4. I don't eat peas anyway! Classroom stories and the
   social construction of childhood
   *Lesley Pugsley, Amanda Coffey and
   Sara Delamont* — 56

5. Growing up respectable — 68
   Odette Parry

6. 'Safe'? Involving children in child protection — 85
   Ian Butler with Howard Williamson

7. Whose life is it anyway? — 107
   Anne Crowley

8.   Accounting for 'child prostitution'   125
        Anne Crowley and Gera Patel

9.   How do young Asian and white people view their
     problems? A step towards child-focused research   142
        Ilan Katz

10. So much for 'participation': Youth work and
     young people   162
        Howard Williamson

List of figures and tables

Figure 6.1	Involving children in child protection	89
Table 9.1	Problems identified	145
Table 9.2	Who would you talk to?	155

Notes on contributors

Ian Butler is Director of Social Work Studies at the University of Wales College, Cardiff. He worked for many years as a social work practitioner in both the voluntary and statutory sectors and as a Parliamentary Research Assistant, prior to taking up his current post. His recent publications include *Children Speak; Children Trauma and Social Work* (Longman 1994) - with Howard Williamson and articles in the *Howard Journal of Criminal Justice, Family Law* and the *International Journal of Family Care*.

Amanda Coffey is a lecturer in the School of Social and Administrative Studies, University of Wales College, Cardiff. She has published in the area of gender and education, occupational socialisation and qualitative research methods. Her recent publications include *Making Sense of Qualitative Data* (1996 Sage) - with Paul Atkinson, and articles in *Gender and Education, Sociology* and in *Qualitative Studies in Education*.

Anne Crowley is a consultant on children's rights and children's advocacy. She was, until 1995, Principal Advocacy Officer with the Children's Society. Based in Wales, her work included policy development around the management of youth crime, institutional care and the provision of advocacy services for young people. Prior to taking up this post in 1989, she worked with young offenders in South East Wales.

Sara Delamont is Reader in Sociology in the School of Social and Administrative Studies at University of Wales College, Cardiff. She is the author of eight books including *Inside the Secondary Classroom* (with M Galton) and editor of eight others. Her main research interests are in the sociology of education.

Ilan Katz received his degree in Social Work at the University of Witwatersrand in Johannesburg in 1978. After qualifying he came to the UK and has worked as a social worker and social work manager in local authorities and voluntary organisations. His current post is National Evaluation Officer for the NSPCC, where he is involved with several projects evaluating child protection practice and has a part-time secondment to the Brunel University Centre for the Evaluation of Public Policy and Practice. His current research interests include comprehensive risk assessment, user empowerment, child witnesses and Area Child Protection Committees. In 1994 he received his doctorate on *The Construction of Racial Identity in Infants of Mixed Parentage* from Brunel University.

Odette Parry has been an undergraduate, a post-graduate and a research fellow at Cardiff. Her research has included work on naturists, journalism students and post-graduates in the natural and social sciences. She is currently a lecturer at the University of the West Indies in Jamaica.

Gera Patel is currently working for the Federation of Black Housing Organisations as a researcher. Previously she worked for the Children's Society who published her work on young people running away from home or care in 1993.

Lesley Pugsley gained her first degree in Sociology and Education at the University of Wales, Cardiff in 1994, then completed an ESRC funded Masters Degree in Social Science research methods. She is currently engaged in ESRC funded PhD research at Cardiff. She is married with three children all of whom are in higher education.

Julie Selwyn is a lecturer in the Family Policy and Child Welfare Centre, in the School of Policy Studies at the University of Bristol. Prior to joining the university she was a social work practitioner, working with children and families in a variety of settings. Her research interests lie in the field of adoption practice, and the views of children about their position in society.

Ian Shaw is Director of Graduate Studies in the School of Social and Administrative Studies at the University of Wales College, Cardiff. His main research activities are in the field of homelessness. His book, *Evaluating in Practice*, published by Ashgate in 1996, reflects his interest in exploring the relationship between understanding and action in professional work.

Howard Williamson is Senior Research Associate in the School of Social and Administrative Studies, University of Wales College, Cardiff. He has written and lectured widely on issues affecting children and young people. His recent publications include *Children Speak* (with Ian Butler), published by Longman 1994, and an edited collection of practice accounts, *Social Action for Young People*, published by Russell House 1995. He is Vice-Chair of the Wales Youth Agency.

Acknowledgements

With grateful acknowledgements to all the children and young people who told us their stories.

1 Children and the sociology of childhood

Ian Butler

Whether in contemplation of the 'new world order' or as a reaction to the excesses of the eighties (expressed as much in house price inflation, apparently, as the horrors of Somalia), the 90's began seemingly full of possibilities for children. The United Nations, in announcing a 'new ethic' as part of the Declaration made at its World Summit on Children held in September 1990, was positively messianic in tone:

> The mental and physical growth of a child cannot be asked to wait until the interest rates fall, or until commodity prices recover, or until debt repayments have been rescheduled, or until the economy returns to growth, or until after a general election, or until a war is over ... In our time, for the first time, we have the chance to begin shielding the lives and the normal growth of children from the worst excesses, misfortunes, and mistakes of the world into which they are born.
>
> (UNICEF 1991: 27)

It has become a commonplace to assert that amongst social scientists too, the horizons are widening and 'new paradigms' are being formed (James and Prout 1991). Complex, multinational research projects such as the 'Childhood as a Social Phenomenon' programme based at the European Centre in Vienna, academic journals sustained wholly on a diet of papers on the sociology of childhood and undergraduate degree schemes that have as their exclusive focus, the study of the child, would seem to mark an exponential growth in interest in children and childhood. And this in such a short space of time.

Quartrup (1994) notes that the 1968 edition of the International Encyclopaedia of the Social Sciences had nothing at all to say about the social life of children. As recently as in 1986, Ambert demonstrated convincingly how little interest the community of social scientists had shown in children thus far and warned any potential recruit to the academic cause that:

> One does not become a household name in sociology by studying children.
>
> (Ambert 1986: 16)

Given the recent and happy alignment of political possibilities and scholarly enthusiasm, it would be easy enough to succumb to the millennial mood and imagine that a new, urgent, emancipatory social science and set of social realities for children was imminent. However, in this field, as elsewhere, we only get the sociology we deserve (or can afford), and along with the New Jerusalem, the 'new paradigm' remains as elusive as ever. What is clear however, is that, irrespective of the social realities of the lives of children and any potential for change that may exist, a re-examination of our appreciation of the cultural facts (La Fontaine 1979) of childhood is required. This chapter will explore the recent history of the study of children as it exemplifies the history of adult myth-making about children, including sociological myth-making, and provides the context in which later chapters in this volume are offered.

Centuries of adulthood

Just as Aries (1960) could claim that in medieval society, the idea of childhood did not exist, one might claim that before Aries, the sociology of childhood did not exist. Late nineteenth and early twentieth century interest in the study of children was predicated on what Hendrick (1994) has called a 'narrative of the body' where the corporeal, rather than the psychological or, much later, the social existence of the child was the object of attention:

> ... when social scientists, philanthropists, doctors, and educationalists and reformers looked at children in the period, say 1870 - 1914, they saw 'bodies' - that is to say that they saw children who were homeless and ragged; infants who were starved, neglected and sometimes murdered by paid carers: children who were hungry; children who were very ill ...
>
> (Hendrick 1994: 3)

The administrative history of the rescue of such children from the pauperism, squalor and disease of the nineteenth century has been well written (Heywood 1969; Pinchbeck and Hewitt 1973) and need not be rehearsed here. Of more relevance to us is the process of transition to a Foucauldian 'narrative of the mind' as fossilised in the corpus of childrearing manuals which were intended to reassure the domestically disadvantaged middle classes and instruct the dangerously inept working classes of the 1930's.

The home front

The mothercraft crusade of the early twentieth century began its conquest of the nursery, in part at least, as a consequence of wars fought elsewhere. The poor physical condition of recruits to the Boer War and the appalling loss of the nation's innocents and innocence in the Great War, spurred a vital interest in defence against the nation's apparent physical vulnerability. In another sense, the struggle was a continuation of the older one against disease, squalor and poverty that left the children of Glasgow or Liverpool still with no more than a fifty-fifty chance of survival in the second decade of the twentieth century and which saw 32,000 children die of diarrhoea in the summer of 1911.

The language of the military and of war is appropriate to the efforts of these stormtroopers of the mothercraft movement and particularly in respect of Dr Frederick Truby King, the undoubted champion of the early exchanges. His rallying cry of 'breast fed is best fed' could send a chill through the staunchest ranks of mothers still daring to feed their infants, via a bottle, on diluted, condensed milk.

For Truby King and the legion of Truby King babies, life was to run with bandbox precision and in parade ground order. Feeding and sleeping was by the clock, at four hourly intervals except at night, when the child would not be fed at all. Potty training was even harsher with results expected within weeks if not days. Unkindest of all, to modern sensibilities, was the denial of physical stimulation to even the youngest child. The advice once given to midwives (and which probably would have been given to social workers, had there been any) which they in turn passed on to the mothers of the current thirty-something generation, reads now like a witness statement drawn up to substantiate allegations of neglect:

> Babies and children, we have been truly told, are all the
> better for a little 'wholesome neglect'. From the beginning

an infant should be trained to spend most of his (sic) time lying alone. He gets quite enough handling while being fed and dressed ... Reserve singing, talking and playing for his (half hour per day) 'playtime: let 'being amused' be a treat - do not let him expect it always, for then he will get no pleasure from it ... Do not point things out to him.

(Frankenburg 1934: 171)

The debilitating consequences for the child's nervous system of being taken for a ride on an omnibus were to be avoided as assiduously as any temptation to thumb sucking or sexual self indulgence (the 'M' word).

The explicit purpose of this particular regime was, in the words of Mabel Liddiard, author of the *Mothercraft Manual* (1928), to engender 'self control, obedience, the recognition of authority, and later, respect for elders'. Such outcomes would be 'essential to the formation of the "normal" stable personality that would form the bedrock of a strong nation' (Humphries and Gordon 1993). The alternative was too awful to contemplate:

The neglected toddler in everyone's way is the material which becomes the disgruntled agitator, while the happy contented child is the pillar of the State.

(St. Aubyn 1935 in Humphries and Gordon 1993)

It is important to catch the echo of these essentially functionalist justifications of childrearing practice as they emerge again in the socialisation theories of the fifties and beyond.

The influence of the Truby King approach must not be overstated, however. The practical domestic arrangements of working class families that necessitated multiple caretaking and which were not susceptible to such oppressive regimentation continued undisturbed in many areas. So too did condensed milk and margarine sandwiches.

Whilst the sheer physicality of the Truby King method is striking, it was not without its psychological grounding. The transformation to the 'narrative of the mind' of the child, what has been called the development of the 'psy complex' (Rose 1985) clearly has its origins here although it awaited its full flowering until the aftermath of the Second World War. The theories of Freud, Adler, Jung and others had begun to exert influence in the twenties, of course, (Hernshaw 1964; Armstrong 1983; Ingelby 1985) but it was not until they were placed in the hands of the professional cadres of the welfare fifties that the maturational processes and transitional significance of childhood really came to be objects of broader social scientific interest. It is only after the child's nature had begun to be 'truly differentiated from that of adults and respected in its own right' (Heywood 1973: 9) that it could be studied as such. Which is not to say that it was, not by sociologists at least. The scientific advantage fell clearly to the psychologists, and in particular to Jean Piaget and his disciples.

Piaget held that intellectual development proceeded in age related stages through an interactive (rather than through a crudely bio-genetic) process of assimilation and accommodation. From learning to interpret sensory information and gaining control of motor skills in the first eighteen months of life to the development of abstract thought and scientific reasoning by age 11, the child moved steadily and predictably towards psychological maturity. Critical in this process, especially in the early years, was the role occupied by the child's primary caretaker, which was conventionally, especially after the popularisation of the work of John Bowlby in the early 1950's, taken to mean the child's mother.

In contrast to the work of Truby King which was to be overwhelmed by ranks of babies left to the more tender mercies of Dr. Spock, the influence of Piaget's work is difficult to overestimate. Both in contemporary 'parent craft' and in education (Walkerdine 1984) Piagetian ideas still constitute professional received wisdom. Even the popular imagination has 'assimilated and accommodated' Piagetian ideas in that children are still frequently 'explained' by reference to the 'phase' that they are going through. Such 'institutionalisation' of particular habits of thought in relation to children represents a formidable barrier to the development of new 'truths' concerning childhood.

The positivist, functionalist sociology of the time, especially in the emerging field of family sociology, provided a suitable context for the development of a comprehensive account of the nature of childhood and the role of children that drew on both of these narratives, that of the body and that of the mind. In the work of Talcott Parsons, for example, the modern family is presented as a structurally isolated, nuclear unit that has shed many of its immediately economic productive functions with its only direct link to economic production maintained through the breadwinning occupational role of the father. The family is primarily a child-rearing and affective unit which serves the 'needs' of the economy by lessening geographical and kinship ties, thus permitting necessary occupational mobility and providing compensatory emotional sanctuary in an otherwise unforgiving world. Within nuclear families, the emotional bonds between spouses and between parents (particularly, mothers) and their children develop and assume a growing social and psychological importance.

Moreover, such affective relationships provide the means whereby cultural and social values are transmitted across the generations. Through a process of *socialisation*, largely in the hands of the child's own family, the child is fitted for whatever social role awaits him or her as an adult:

> Within the family ... with its powerful natural ties of affection, is found the most abundantly and most exclusively the power to teach the child behaviour, self discipline, values and the code of society. The whole art of living is interpreted and handed on to the child by his parent ...
>
> (Heywood 1970: 139)

The child's physical well-being, its psychological growth, the art and craft of parenting and their combined value to the wider society combine powerfully in the several variants of socialisation theory. Socialisation theory's utility and explanatory potential was increased even further however, by its absorption into the welfare apparatus of the fifties.

Children of the state

Public interest in the domestic life of the child in the fifties drew its strength from at least two distinct sources, both having a common origin in the Second World War. Firstly, the War had, through evacuation, for example, brought about considerable disruption in patterns of family life. Women in the labour force, fathers readjusting to family life after considerable absences in some cases and a sharp rise in illegitimacy identified the child and the family as potential beneficiaries of the welfarism of the late forties and early fifties.

Secondly, there was considerable parliamentary interest in the apparent failures of both the legislative framework and the practical arrangements available to deal effectively with the problems of the increased number of children in the public care. Predicated on the Poor Law Act of 1930, for example, in 1947, the duty of the local authority to the destitute child beyond 'giving them relief':

> ... was still only 'to set (them) to work or to put (them) out as apprentices', though they are empowered in the cold words of the Act ... to establish separate schools for 'the relief and management of the children to be received therein.'
>
> (S. Clement Brown in Dyson 1947: iii)

Clement Brown's purpose is to form the contrast between apparent legislative intent and the concerns of her own time. Her case had been made more urgent by the death, in 1945, of 11 year old Denis O'Neil whilst in foster care. This had prompted the establishment of the Curtis Committee which gave close scrutiny to existing arrangements for children in institutional care too:

> We found in fact many [Homes] where the standard of child care was no better ... than that of thirty years ago ... in many Homes [there] was a lack of personal interest in and affection for the children which we found shocking. The child in these Homes was not recognised as an individual with his own rights and possessions, his own life to live and his own contribution to offer. He was merely one of a crowd ... Still more important, he was without the feeling that there was anyone to whom he could turn who was vitally interested in his welfare or who cared for him as a person.
>
> (Curtis Committee 1946)

One might note that for Dyson and others at the time, the solution, when return to the child's 'natural family' proved impossible, lay in the development of foster care, where the magic of the family might still have scope to work (Butler and Owens 1993).

The growing ranks of child care professionals developed other technologies too. Actual and potential failures in socialisation gave rise to unlimited opportunities to intervene in the lives of families and their children. Delinquency, poor educational attainment, failing personal relationships could all be understood as the consequences of inadequate socialisation and therefore be susceptible to the ministrations of the minor professional from the local authority. Most insidious of all though was the normative tendency of socialisation theories that could find and explain problems in the every day lives of certain groups of children and therefore justify the imposition of solutions:

> socialisation consists of the processes through which, by one method or another, children are made to conform, in cases of 'successful' socialisation or become deviants in cases of 'failed' socialisation.
>
> (Shildkrout 1978: 109ff.)

The experimental underpinning of Piaget's work was being seriously questioned by the early seventies (Modgil and Modgil 1982; Sutherland 1992). Talcott Parsons' underlying assumptions and analysis had long been suffering the same fate too (Gordon 1972; Morgan 1975). But the persistent and ultimately fatal flaw in functionalist socialisation theories, irrespective of the particular sources from which they draw their intellectual justification, lies in their fundamental confusion over the subject of sociological and psychological theorising. Psychology understands the individual as an instance of the species whereas sociology understands the individual as an instance of the society. Hence, the 'facts' of biological growth neither do nor can predict the 'facts' of life in society which is negotiated in the context of social relations (Jenks 1982).

Nonetheless, one can clearly see in the words of the Curtis Committee, reported above, albeit securely located within the family, a clear sense of the differentiation and respect for childhood as a social form that is a prerequisite of its serious study. Such accounts and the developments in social policy that were justified by them, however speciously, did produce substantial material improvements in the social circumstances of most children (Pugh 1993).

Nothing can hide the fact however, that such functionalist socialisation theories presume a deficit model of childhood. That is to say that childhood is understood only as a transitional process, en route to becoming adult. It is a state of becoming, not one of being. Socialisation is, in Thorne's words, 'ahistorical, individualist, and teleological' (Thorne 1985: 696). Moreover, of much more enduring significance is the consequent (but not inevitable) assumption that childhood is therefore 'less' than adulthood. The value of childhood lies, in such accounts, in its simultaneous use as preparation for adulthood and its capacity to ensure the stability of cultural and social reproduction. No sociology that takes seriously the study of children of and for themselves can rest on such foundations.

Aries and all that

Although Aries' *Centuries of Childhood* was not the first substantial critique of contemporary accounts of childhood, it enjoys something of the status of an epoch making event. Aries' original thesis concerning the discovery and gradual diffusion of childhood between the fifteenth and the eighteenth centuries is of less enduring importance (See Pollock 1983; Archard 1993) than the contribution he made to the development of what

Prout and James have called the 'theoretically plausible space called the social construction of childhood' (James and Prout 1991: 27).

Evidence of the cultural specificity of childhood had been available since the nineteen twenties and thirties in the work of social anthropologists such as Mead and Benedict. However, their work had been pressed into service to illustrate the universality of the processes of socialisation and its role in cultural transmission and reproduction rather than to question it.

Aries' fortune was to publish in a changing intellectual climate that coincided with the recent (on the European side of the Atlantic), exponential growth in interest in an interpretivist tradition in sociological thought. Interactionism and phenomenology in particular, with their concern for the meaning rather than the function of social events and processes, presented a fundamental challenge to prevailing functionalist, socialisation theories. The challenge lay in questioning the implicit assumption in such functionalist (and normative) accounts that no social category, including childhood, was either fixed or unitary but re-negotiated daily between social actors - including children. That children might, at least in part, be self-conscious authors of their own biography is perhaps best developed in relation to the activities of their older brothers and sisters, in the sociology of youth and in particular in the sociology of delinquent youth.

In characterising this relational account of the locus of young people in society, caution must be exercised in illustrating from the work of American criminologists of this period. For Merton (1964), for example, delinquency was the consequence of frustrated access to social, cultural and material rewards. For David Matza (1961) delinquency involved the inappropriate expression of widely shared but subterranean values. Although Miller's work recognises more explicitly the conflict of interest between the values held by certain groups of young people and the dominant cultural and social interests, it is to the work of the New Criminologists on this side of the Atlantic that we should look for continued relevance.

Built on a tradition of Marxist thought, it is the achievement of the 'new criminologists' (Taylor, Walton and Young 1973) to include in the sociology of youth the sociological variable of class. Although, in a sense, the intrusion of the class variable, still accounts for children (or at least older children) only in relation to pre-existing, adult 'truths' about the social world, children are seen, really for the first time, to be real actors in that world. For, by demonstrating that the rituals of deviant youth were a form of real resistance (Hall and Jefferson 1976) the 'new criminologists' demonstrated the potential and the potency of young people as social beings:

> sub-cultures are not simply 'ideological' constructs. They too, win space for the young: cultural space in the neighbourhood and institutions, real time for leisure and recreation, actual room on the street or street-corner, They serve to mark out an appropriate 'territory' in the localities. They focus around key occasions of social interaction: the week-end, the disco, the bank-holiday trip, the night-out at the 'centre', and 'stand-about-doing-nothing' of the weekday evening, the Saturday match.

The possibility that younger children might also occupy semi-autonomous social worlds where their behaviour and language was neither asocial or pre-rational did not develop at this time as fully as one might have anticipated. Although in the field of education (Heath 1983; Cook-Gumperz, Corsaro & Streeck 1986), work in the early seventies did suggest a shift away from the adult constructions of the role and purpose of education to the expressed meanings it had for its subjects (see also Pugsley, Coffey and Delamont later in this volume).

Emancipation

Elsewhere, the literature of the time still echoes the relative powerlessness and subject nature of childhood. Holt's 1975 liberationist 'manifesto' *Escape From Childhood* describes the state of childhood as:

> being wholly subservient and dependent ... being seen by others as a mixture of expensive nuisance, slave and super-pet.

> (Holt 1975: 15)

He goes on to describe family life as a 'training for slavery' sustained by the far from disinterested motives of parents who need their children as love objects as much as they need each other as sex objects.

This association of the emancipatory progress of women with the experience of childhood produced some striking rhetoric in the mid-seventies around the contemporary lot of children. The American feminist,

Shulamith Firestone, saw in the 'myth of childhood' a way for adults to compensate for all the things that are or were missing from their own lives.

> ....it is every parent's duty to give his child a childhood to remember (swing sets, inflated swimming pools, toys and games, camping trips, birthday parties, etc.)
>
> (Firestone 1979, 40)

And she enjoins us to:

> ....talk about what childhood is really like and not of what it is like in adult heads... In a culture of alienated people, the belief that everyone has at least one good period in life free of care and drudgery dies hard. And obviously you can't expect it in old age. So it must be you've already had it. This accounts for the fog of sentimentality surrounding any discussion of childhood or children. Everyone is living out some private dream on their behalf.
>
> (p.42)

The relationship between academic feminism and the sociology of childhood is not a simple alliance however. The construction of motherhood as part of 'women's work' in the eighties, whilst elevating the status of the nurturing function (Gordon 1982) and forming the basis of an unarguable case for the wider recognition and public support for the domestic labour of women (Maroney 1986), still tended to objectify children; to treat them as the objects of mothering. Later deconstruction of motherhood and its location in a set of gendered relations and a:

> sexist ideology that had represented maternity, life with children and the labour of child care as women's ahistorical and natural destiny.

still presented children

> as objects with needs, translated into demands for care. Therefore, in this type of analysis, children have merely functioned as the instruments by which patriarchal society reproduces prevailing gender arrangements that feminists seek to transform.
>
> (Alanen 1994: 33 ff.)

It is Alanen's contention however, that the traditional exclusion from 'the proper domain of sociology' of women and children have parallels and that any new sociology of childhood can profit from the experience of academic feminism.

She characterises early academic feminism as asking 'the woman question' in and of the social sciences. The systematic inclusion of the 'sex/gender' variable and a focus on 'women's issues' irrevocably made women more visible within social scientific discourse, she argues. Indeed, there is some evidence, particularly in the interest in individual civil rights (Franklin 1986), that the 'child question' is being more frequently asked in areas once reserved exclusively for adults:

> the irrationality and immorality of systematic and institutionalised discrimination against individuals on the basis of their gender or race has, to some degree been established ... equivalent discrimination against people on the basis of their age has proven more resilient to change.
>
> (Franklin 1986: 1)

In this respect, the contemporary state of the study of childhood can be likened to the 'jumping off point' of more recent feminist perspectives in sociological thought.

The 'child question' (as was the 'woman question') is, however, essentially revisionist and, as such, inevitably insufficient. It helps to understand the social realities of children and childhood according to the standpoint of a science that is fundamentally 'adultist'. In the same way that social events and processes are 'gendered', might they not also be 'generationed'? Thus those aspects of the social lives of children which are the focus of scientific attention are essentially those that concern

> ... organising, managing, regulating and occasional modernising of the generational system from the standpoint of those belonging to the hegemonic generation ...
>
> (Alanen 1994: 38)

If sociology is situated knowledge, a true sociology of childhood would describe society therefore from the standpoint of the child. It is this which represents the dynamic potential for a credible, new sociology of childhood.

A new sociology of childhood?

How then does one study children from their own standpoint? How are children to be studied in their own right and not just as 'receptacles of adult teaching' (Hardman 1973: 87)?

> What a children's standpoint therefore means is, that researchers by means of scientific instruments describe, explain and interpret aspects of children's life world. In terms of describing children's life conditions the demand is to use children as our unit of observation and as *mediators of information* ... Children have much to say themselves, their daily actions and practice can be read and interpreted so as to add to our knowledge about their own life and arenas ... The general suspicion towards children's credibility as witnesses about their own life - and even about adult's life and society at all - should be critically reassessed.
>
> (Quartrup 1994 (p. 6) emphasis added.)

This volume attempts to take a further modest step towards such a sociology by contributing additional accounts of such worlds, largely in children's own words. The methodological difficulties of gathering such accounts are formidable and are explored by Shaw below, yet they do not appear insuperable. Of more substance, is the question of the interpretation of such accounts. The epistemological contradiction between the production of knowledge concerning children by adults (children remain the only group that do not undertake their own research) is, as yet, unresolved. Presently, we may need to be content with a

> weaker sense of authenticity in which previously unexplored or unreported aspects of childhood are made available and previously mute children empowered to speak ...
>
> (James and Prout 1991: 27)

More positively, it is possible to outline other essential dimensions of a sociology of childhood from a child's standpoint. For example, such a sociology needs to establish a different relationship with family sociology. Growing awareness of and interest in the family as the site, not only of parental nurture but also of parental exploitation of children for economic as well as sexual gratification clearly argues for a differentiation of the interests of adults and children in thinking about families.

As well as being relational, such a sociology will also be structural in its analytical orientation. This is to recognise that childhood is a persistent social form. Whilst individual children grow up and out of childhood, others take their place and continue to occupy a recognisable social category or form. Thus childhood can be studied intergenerationally: how do the social significance and life circumstances of children vary in relation to those of other age groups? Childhood can also be studied interculturally: how does childhood in one country compare with that in another? Childhood can also be studied historically: how do larger historical processes impact on children and the experience of childhood. It may be necessary to argue, as Quartrup does (Quartrup 1994) that children studied in this way, as a 'collectivity', can not allow of too much internal differentiation, by gender, for example, but that remains an open question.

Conclusion

Mention has already been made of the way in which the institutionalisation of hegemonic 'truths' about childhood make the production of other 'truths' problematic. The history of the study of childhood is the history of adults' study of childhood. Any adult conception of childhood seems to be constructed quite differently to how childhood itself was experienced or is currently being lived, by definition. Either that or the collective attention span is very short to judge by how frequently we are prepared to be shocked by what research into childhood actually tells us.

Despite there being no study to our knowledge that reports the social world of children to be a relatively simple and comprehensible place, we seem unprepared to acknowledge the maturity and sophistication that children bring to their understanding of the world and their place in it (Coles 1967, 1986; Denzin 1977). We seem equally unprepared for the realities, sordid or otherwise, of children's lives, whether this be in terms of sexuality (Fine 1981; Martinson 1981), drug use (Adler and Adler 1978), aggression (Fine 1987) or in terms of social and cultural reproduction (Willis 1978).

There is little reason to believe that current adult interest in children and childhood is substantively different from that which it has always been. The 'quiet catastrophe' that sees 40,000 children a day dying from malnutrition and disease, a further 150 million ill and untreated and 100 million denied an education continues uninterrupted. Adult interest in children remains either, at best, secondary or, at worst, self-interest.

This is the real challenge for any new paradigm of the sociology of childhood; how to make it a sociology not just *about* children but also to make it one *for* them. This book is intended as a contribution to such an endeavour.

References

Adler, P. and P. Adler (1978), 'Tinydopers: A Case Study of Deviant Socialization', *Symbolic Interaction* 1:90-105.

Alanen, L. (1994), 'Gender and Generation: Feminism and the 'Child Question' in *Childhood Matters: Social Theory, Practice and Politics*, Qvortrup, J., Bardy, M., Sgritta, G and Wintersberger, H. (eds.) Aldershot: Avebury.

Ambert, A.M. (1986), 'The Place of Children in North American Sociology' in *Sociological Studies in Child Development*, Adler P. and Adler P. (eds.), Greenwich (Conn.), JAI Press.

Archard, D. (1993), *Children - Rights and Childhood*, London: Routledge.

Aries, P. (1960), *L'Enfant et la vie familiale sous l'ancien regime*, Paris: Libraire Plon, Translated by Robert Baldick as 'Centuries of Childhood' (1962), London: Jonathan Cape.

Armstrong D. (1983), *The Political Anatomy of the Body: Medical Knowledge in Britain in the Twentieth Century*, London: Warburg Institute.

Butler, I. and D. Owens (1993), 'Canaries Among Sparrows - Ideas of the Family and the Practice of Foster Care' *International Journal of Family Care*, Vol. 5, 25-42.

Coles, R. (1967), *Children of Crisis*, Boston USA: Little, Brown.

Cook-Gumperz J., Corsaro, W.A. & Streeck, J. (eds) (1986), *Children's Worlds and Children's Language*, Berlin: Mouton de Gruyter.

Curtis Committee (1946), *Report of the Care of Children Committee*, Cmnd. 6922 London: HMSO.

Denzin, N.K. (1977), *Childhood Socialization*, San Francisco: Jossey-Bass.

Dyson, D. M. (1947), *The Foster Home and the Boarded Out Child*, London: George Allen and Unwin.

Fine, G. (1981), 'Friends, Impression Management and Pre-adolescent Behaviour', in S. Asher and J. Gottman (eds), *The Development of Children's Friendships*, Cambridge: Cambridge University Press.

Fine, G. (1987), *With the Boys*, Chicago: Chicago Press.

Firestone, S. (1979), 'Childhood is Hell', in M. Hoyles (ed.) (1979), *Changing Childhood*, London: Writers and Readers Publishing Co-operative.

Frankenburg, S. (1934), *Common Sense in the Nursery*, London: Cape.

Franklin, B. (ed.) (1986), *The Rights of Children*, London: Blackwell.

Gordon, L. (1982), 'Why the Nineteenth-Century Feminists Did Not Support 'Birth Control' and twentieth-Century feminists Do: Feminism, Reproduction and the Family' in Thorne, B and Yalom, M. (eds) *Rethinking the Family. Some Feminist Questions*, New York: Longman.

Gordon, M. (1972), *The Nuclear Family in Crisis: The Search for an Alternative*, New York: Harper and Row.

Hall. S & Jefferson, T. (1976), *Resistance through Rituals*, London: Hutchinson.

Hardman, C. (1973), 'Can There Be an Anthropology of Children?' *Journal of the Anthropological Society of Oxford*, Vol. 4:1 pp. 85 - 99.

Heath, S.B., (1983), *Ways with Words: Language, Life and Work in Communities and Classrooms*, Cambridge: CUP.

Hendrick, H. (1994), *Child Welfare - England 1972 - 1989*, London: Routledge.

Hernshaw, L.S. (1964), *A Short History of British Psychology: 1840 - 1940*, London: Methuen.

Heywood, J.S. (1969), *Childhood and Society 100 Years Ago*, London: National Children's Home.

Heywood, J.S. (1970), *Child in Care*, 2nd ed., London: RKP.

Heywood, J.S. (1973), 'Services for Children and their Families' in Stroud, J. (ed.) *Services for Children and their Families: Aspects of Child Care for Social Workers*, London: Pergammon Press.

Holt, J. (1975), *Escape from Childhood. The Needs and Rights of Children*, London: Penguin.

Humphries, S. & Gordon, P. (1993), *Labour of Love: The Experience of Parenthood in Britain 1900 - 1950*, London: Sidgwick and Jackson.

Ingelby, D. (1985), 'Professionals as Socialisers: the 'Psy Complex' in Scull, A. and Spitzer, S. (eds.) *Research in Law, Deviance and Social Control* New York: JAI Press.

James, A and Prout, A. (1991), 'A New Paradigm for the Sociology of Childhood? Provenance, Promise and Problems' in James, A and Prout, A. (eds) *Constructing and Reconstructing Childhood: Contemporary Issues in the Sociological Study of Childhood*, London: The Falmer Press.

Jenks, C. (1982), *The Sociology of Childhood: Essential Readings*, London: Batsford.

La Fontaine, J.S. (1979), *Sex and Age as Principles of Social Differentiation*, London: Academic Press.

Liddiard, M. (1928), *Mothercraft Manual*, London.

Maroney, R.M. (1986), *Shared Responsibility - Families and Social Policy*, New York: Aldine de Gruyter.

Martinson, F. (1981), 'Preadolescent Sexuality - Latent or Manifest?', in L. Constantine and F.M. Martinson, *Children and Sex*, Boston: Little, Brown.

Matza, D. (1961), 'Subterranean traditions of youth' *Annals of the American Academy of Political and Social Science*, 338, 102-18.

Merton, R.K. (1964), 'Anomie, anomia and social interaction' in Clinnard, M.B. (ed.) *Anomie and Deviant Behaviour*, New York, Free Press.

Modgil, S. and Modgil, C. (eds) (1982), *Jean Piaget: Consensus and Controversy*, Eastbourne: Holt, Rinehart and Winston.

Morgan D.J. (1975), *Social Theory and the Family*, London: RKP.

Pinchbeck, I. and Hewitt, M. (1973), *Children in English Society*, London: RKP.

Pollock, L. (1983), *Forgotten Children. Parent-child relations from 1500 - 1900*, Cambridge: Cambridge University Press.

Pugh, G. (ed) (1993), *30 Years of Change for Children*, London: National Children's Bureau.

Quartrup, J (1994), 'Recent Developments in Research and Thinking on Childhood' Paper at the XXXI International Sociological Association Committee on Family Research, London: 28th - 30th April 1994.

Rose, N. (1985), *The Psychological Complex: Psychology, Politics and Society in England 1869 - 1939*, London: RKP.

Shildkrout, E. (1978), 'Roles of Children in Urban Kano' in La Fontaine, J.S. *Sex and Age as Principles of Social Differentiation*, London: Academic Press.

St. Aubyn, G. (1935), *Family Book*, London.

Sutherland, P. (1992), *Cognitive Development Today - Piaget and his Critics*, London: Paul Chapman.

Taylor, I. Walton, P. and Young, J. (1973), *The New Criminology - For a Sociology of Deviance*, London: RKP.

Thorne, B. (1985), 'Putting a Price on Children' *Contemporary Sociology* Vol 14. No. 6 p, 695 - 696.

UNICEF (1991), *The State of the World's Children*, Oxford: Oxford University Press.

Walkerdine, V. (1984), 'Developmental Psychology and the Child-centered Pedagogy: The Insertion of Piaget into Early Education' in Henriques, J. *et al* (eds) *Changing the Subject: Psychology, Social Regulation and Subjectivity,* London: Methuen.

Willis, P. (1978), *Learning to Labour: How working class kids get working class jobs*, Farnborough: Saxon House.

2 Unbroken voices: Children, young people and qualitative methods

Ian Shaw

The hallmark of this book is a sociology of childhood expressed through a series of illustrations of the ways in which a *qualitative* sociology enriches our understanding of childhood. Furthermore, this is not only a qualitatively grounded sociology *about* children but one in which the voices of children and young people are directly heard pulled taut against the voices of adults. It is both a sociology *of* children and childhood, and a sociology *for* children and childhood. 'Children and childhood' is no accident. There is no homogeneous 'childhood', just as there is no undifferentiated qualitative method waiting to be applied to childhood. To assume so would be to run the risk of the sociological sadism against which Robert Merton warned, when the interests of the person are swallowed in the abstractions of the sociologist. There is a plurality of childhoods. But having said this we are equally opposed to disaggregating our understanding of childhood, such that the unique 'child' erases the common characteristics and rights of children.

There is no tradition within sociology for studying childhood. Work in this field only began in the 1980's, although major initiatives such as the Childhood as a Social Phenomenon project at the European Centre in Vienna (Qvortrup, Bardy, Sgritta and Wintersberger, 1994), benchmark collections of readings (James and Prout, 1990; Waksler, 1991), and evidence of continuing interest in micro-level studies of children's lives (Mayall, 1994), demonstrate the considerable distance that has been travelled over a short time. Qualitative sociologists are not alone in their concern for children's voices and rights to be heard. Saporitti, Qvortrup and Hernandez have made effective cases regarding the 'conceptual and numerical marginalisation of children' (Qvortrup, 1990: 80) and against the bias of social statistics (Saporitti, 1994) - bias both in the ways social statistics are assembled and the uses to which they are put. Saporitti demonstrates the ways in which our social accounting systems make childhood invisible. In many governmental statistics children do not count either as units of observation or as units for analysis.

Saporitti illustrates the potential for exploiting statistics to present a very different picture in which the child becomes central. We lack 'a systematic and coherent set of demographic, social and economic indicators appropriate for assessing the social status of childhood in contemporary industrial societies' (p190). He is committed wholeheartedly to a theoretically driven attempt to provide empirical support for a new sociology of childhood, and not just to the collection of new statistics. He applies this strategy to statistics dealing with population structure, dependency ratios, family statistics, poverty and fertility. For example, he charts the ratio between children and elderly people. Instead of seeing this statistic as an indicator of the problem of ageing populations he sees it as a 'co-existence ratio' - a measure of the shifting balance and relationship between the elderly and children. On fertility statistics he observes that 'all theories advanced to explain the decline in fertility consider children a "dependent variable" in a world of adults: in other words, all these theories focus on adults' (p209). He invites us to consider whether there may be a relationship between the decline in fertility and images of childhood, and whether the decline in fertility will mean lower status for children or children being treated as a precious social good.

Saporitti and Hernandez (1995) provide radical and persuasive example of an argument for a *quantitative* approach in which a sociography of childhood is central. Yet it does not and cannot go far enough. At the purely pragmatic level, official statistics are very rarely child based (ie the unit of collection is not the child, and the analysis is not about children), and this limits the extent to which a creative re--reading of this kind can be carried out. Statistics on children vary greatly in availability, quality, scope, and comparability across time, and often provide a one-sided emphasis on the family and material circumstances of children (Brannen and O'Brian, 1995). Comparative analysis across time and space is difficult. Saporitti admits that

> Thus we are often compelled to resort to methodological and
> technical devices that frequently leave us with 'artefacts'
> rather than well grounded and valid indicators of childhood
> status
>
> (Saporiti, 1994: 195).

There are more significant limitations. The method inevitably yields an adult perspective, which does not require any direct understanding of the child's own view. In addition, at its best it poses interesting questions which can be tabled but not resolved. Butler has already made the point that changing ratios of children to older people may or may not indicate changing *relationships* between people across the generations (cf Pilcher, 1995). Social demography will not give us sufficient answers.

A growing interest in qualitative studies of children has led to a shift away from traditional methods such as experiments and hypothesis testing strategies. Qualitative studies fall into two broad clusters. The identification of consistent trends and stages in children's development within social, family and educational contexts has provided the thrust for many studies, and has influenced the work reported here by Parry and by Pugsley, Coffey and Delamont. Selwyn's poignant account in chapter three of the disappointed efforts of childless couples to adopt underscores the depth to which norms of parenthood can confound careers of family lives. More typically associated with qualitative work has been the second cluster of studies 'involving naturalistic observation and micro-ethnography where the focus is on discovering and describing stable features of children's life-worlds' (Corsaro and Streeck, 1986: 29). One area of growth has been ethnographies of pre-school years (eg Corsaro, 1985; Mandell, 1988), which served to bring to the fore the way in which previous studies had overemphasised development processes at the expense of direct consideration of what the events of everyday life look like in childhood. These studies also served to show, by way of contrast, how researchers, with occasional exceptions (eg Denzin, 1977), had tended to remove themselves from the social context of children's peer activities.

Studies of children fall into three kinds (Fine and Sandstrom, 1988). There are those that find children to be more mature or capable than we have expected. Fine and Sandstrom conclude that they 'know of no study that has found that children are more "childish" than we have given them credit for' (p72), though they admit this could be the product of social science ideologies, in which researchers want to make their work important by showing their informants are talented. The work described here by Crowley, and also the analysis of children's involvement in prostitution, by Crowley and Patel, illustrate this tradition of social research. Second, there are studies that find children and young people to be more tendentious and rebellious - studies that act in effect to deromanticise childhood. In contrast with American research, British research has often been about working class youth. The work of people such as Paul Willis (1978) has addressed the problem of how the class system is produced, and is more broadly theoretical than American work. Williamson describes research with young people in the British youth services in a later chapter of this book which is influenced by this tradition. Finally, there are those studies that have shed light on how socialisation by peers occurs among children and young people. Much of this work has been done in the context of schooling, setting a secret process of education alongside formal schooling (eg Bowles and Gintis, 1976). Parry's account in this volume of participant observation in naturist clubs considers socialisation processes in a different setting.

The work of Piaget and Kohlberg has been foremost in casting an image of childhood marked by a series of developmental stages. From the perspective of mainline, functional socialisation theories, qualitative work with children is viewed as finding age-appropriate ways for the 'knowing' adult to learn about children. The special nature of research methods with children is regarded as stemming from the limited extents to which children are able to comprehend language, articulate subjective experience and sustain affective relationships (eg Parker, 1984). This deficit model surfaces in the ways researchers worry to their readers about doing research. For example, Bierman and Schwartz's account of clinical interviews warns that pre-school children

> *have trouble* holding more than one concept at a time in mind. Additionally, their conceptions are *limited* to ideas that can take concrete, observable forms. They are *unable* to consider alternative perspectives ... They are *just learning* how to interpret others' emotions
>
> (Bierman and Schwartz, 1986: 268, emphasis added)

There are disturbing consequences of a deficit model of this kind for the understanding of the cultures of children. Indeed, children are unlikely to be seen as having their own culture, or at most that culture will be seen according to how closely it approximates the culture and world of adults. Criticism of this position has steadily grown. Jenks rejects the influence of Piaget and also that of Talcott Parsons as a form of ethnocentrism in which

> the continuous lived social practice of being a child ... is ignored. This unilateral manipulation of the child within socialisation theories condemns him to be an absent presence, a nominal cipher without an active dimension
>
> (Jenks, 1992: 13)

One of the major forces initiating a welcome corrective to this research was the work of Cicourel on children's language (1974), which presented a view of children as capable of having their own culture, generationally transmitted by children. Pugsley's chapter illustrates the kind of understanding that emerges from studies of this kind. On this very different view of children they are seen to possess interpretive competence equal to or even greater than adults, and as being potentially 'more creative, more honest, in short, in some ways more human than adults' (Goode, 1986: 84). This challenges the mainstream assumption that adult intervention is essential in order to gain competence. Goode regards the model of children as *tabula rasa*, growing in developmental stages, as an ethnocentric 'adultism' in which researchers reveal themselves as parents writing slightly abstract versions of their own or other peoples' children - a concern reflected in Butler and Williamson's chapter.

It does not need saying that there are diverse cultures of childhood just as there are of adulthood. Age, social class, ethnic identity and, beyond a certain age, gender all pattern the cultures of childhood. Indeed, we would not wish to pose a stark choice of culture *versus* developmental stages. It is not either/or. We must accept children's world views as a legitimate, lived reality, and yet also accept the significance of the constant change and growing that occurs in childhood. Parry's work described in this book how ideas of culture and development may mutually enrich our understanding of children.

Unfortunately participation in 'Kid Society' (the term is Glassner's) is not guaranteed to all who are young. Not all children attain to being a kid. 'It is possible to undergo the physical processes of growth and maturation which we associate with childhood without ever becoming a kid' (Goode, 1986: 88). Goode's work and relationship with Christina, a profoundly deaf-blind child, in which he used 'mimicking, remaining passively obedient during interaction, prolonged observation, video-taping interaction and simulated deaf-blind experiences' (p94), demonstrate how 'adultcentric' research can be transformed, and how he 'had become her student in order to become her tutor' (p100).

Understanding children

Understanding the world of understanding children pulls with both fascination and mystification. How many of us have delved into Iona and Peter Opie's books both to learn and to recall (eg Opie and Opie, 1959; 1969; cf Opie and Opie, 1991)? Our 'problem' with children's society is their closeness and social distance. 'Our proximity to children may lead us to believe that we are closer to them than we really are - only differing in that ... children are still growing up ... and they are often wrong' (Fine and Sandstrom, 1988: 34). This is the problem of ethnocentrism to which Goode refers, though it is made worse by the fact that we do not recognise it as problematic.

Can we understand children? My own answer to this question is 'Yes, but our understandings, though real, will always be approximate and provisional'. 'The participation of our youth leaves a permanent door to kids' culture. There is a Peter Pan in each of us' (Goode, 1986: 101). Siegert takes a similar position in his valuable reflections on the paradox of adults interviewing children. While he thinks the possibility of adults understanding children cannot sensibly be denied, he acknowledges the possibility that

> children reveal in contexts of peer activity social competences which differ from the interviewer's 'model of the competent speaker' and, therefore, remain uninterpreted or are, at worst, not even admitted as displays of social competence
>
> (Siegert, 1986: 367)

This links to a problem evident throughout qualitative sociology, which is how we account for thinking-as-usual, taken for granted knowledge. Good ethnographies display tacit knowledge, described by Altheide and Johnson as 'the largely unarticulated, contextual understanding that is often manifested in nods, silences, humour and naughty nuances'. Tacit knowledge exists 'in that time when action is taken that is not understood, when understanding is offered without articulation, and when conclusions are apprehended without an argument' (Altheide and Johnson, 1994: 492). This is a special issue in research with young children, where the evidence suggests that children rely less on precise verbal explications and concentrate more on non-verbal cues. Thus, while adults may often describe children's talk as 'babbling',

> Unintelligible noise is both part of children's involvement with each other and a device to exclude adults from their play. Children often do no understand others' precise meanings. They require less detail and specification to create acts
>
> (Mandell, 1988: 449)

In circumstances where 'shared meanings, perhaps only roughly understood' are sufficient, and where children have the ability to filter out irrelevant sound and monitor and anticipate adult intrusions, tacit knowing takes on a particular form which may be all the more difficult for adults, and children themselves, to elicit. The social age of children is relevant to this point. With pre-school children, for example, the problem of knowing their culture is especially difficult. For children approaching adolescence with its associated transitions, the worlds of meaning of adulthood and childhood overlap, and that overlap will be a central focus of interpretation. By adolescence, 'the game of life is being played for keeps even when the players find the rules somewhat obscure' (Fine and Sandstrom, 1988: 60). Age begins to be less important in differentiating oneself, and class, gender and race become still more important. Katz' account of groups of Asian young people in chapter nine conveys this point.

Because of these changing worlds it is relevant to ask if young people understand children, and to be aware of the implications of asking older children and young people to reflect back on their recollections of their own childhoods. At this point there is common ground between qualitative sociology with children, young people and adults. Qualitative work with children should be regarded as a process of narrative inquiry. Children are both living their stories in an experiential text, but also telling their stories as they talk to their own selves and explain themselves to others. We may describe this as a simultaneous process of 'storying' and 'restorying' (Connelly and Clandinin, 1990). The thrust of a qualitative strategy is to make these neighbours into strangers and thence into peers, if we are to obtain a sense of what it means to be a child, and be able to view the world 'through their hearts and minds'. In doing so we struggle to mine our own experience, and will be challenged to breach our well constructed defences. It is not without its rewards. 'While children are constructing their own worlds, they sometimes permit us to stand with them to enjoy the monuments they have made' (Fine and Sandstrom, 1988: 76-77).

Our claim that we can understand children in ways which are real if approximate and provisional needs further defence. Are we not living in a world of socially constructed actions? On what grounds do we assert this degree of realism in our accounts of childhood? One of the recurring themes of this book is about how people understand and respond to social problems. There are two broad options on offer in deciding what is intended by a 'social problem'. We may describe these as the *objectivist* option and the *constructivist* one. For the objectivist, a social problem is a social condition that is widely regarded as undesirable, has been caused by the actions or inactions of people, and is thought to effect a relatively large

25

number of people. This view fits commonsense definitions of social problems, but raises two difficulties. First, it minimises or even denies the subjective dimension. It fails to take into account that a social problem is such because enough people *believe* it to be so. Child prostitution, the experiences of children in their families, schooling, and so on, may come to be regarded as social problems without there being any necessary alteration in the social condition. Second, objectivist definitions leave us with no way of seeing what different social problems have in common (Best, 1989).

Constructivist perspectives focus on the processes by which some people designate some social condition as a problem. In other words, social problems are understood in terms of a series of claims-making activities. Hence, social problems refer to two very different things from each perspective. For the objectivist social problems are social conditions. For the constructivist, social problems are claims making activities, and the social conditions may be of little interest in their own right. A given social condition may be construed as several different social problems. Child prostitution, for instance, may be seen as a problem about policing, male oppression, the breakdown of family life or welfare state provision for homeless people. Crowley and Patel discuss some of the consequences of this claims making process in this book.

The stances of contributors to this book are by and large unsympathetic to objectivist perspectives, but neither can they be labelled simply as constructivist. A common sense reading of most of these chapters probably will lead the reader to conclude that the writers believe the views and perspectives of the children and young people to whom they spoke are more true to reality in some ways than adult accounts. This of course poses a tricky point for constructivists. Do they see the world as entirely constructed - and therefore without any knowable connection to 'real' social conditions - or are qualitative accounts in some significant sense better stories about how the world really is? Is a social problem a process whereby meanings come to be shared, accepted or disputed, or is it also some kind of plausible statement about actual social conditions?

Best helpfully distinguishes between *strict* constructivists and *contextual* constructivists (Best, 1989: 243-253). Strict constructivists accept entirely the distinction between knowable claims and unknowable social conditions, and in consequence refuse to make any assumptions about the real world. The difficulty with this position is that it does not sit comfortably with most qualitative research, including the research described in this volume. Constructivists often appear to be making a case along the lines that *new* and *unwarranted* claims are being made - unwarranted because insufficient grounds, warrants and conclusions (Best,

1987) have been evidenced to make a persuasive case. Best believes that such a case can be justified in terms of contextual constructivism. Qualitative sociologists of this ilk accept that they are making some assumptions about social conditions. 'Contextual constructionists argue that any claim can be evaluated ... (they) assume that they can know - with reasonable confidence - about social conditions' (Best, 1989: 247). It is possible, albeit imperfectly, to know the social context in which claims are made.

Contextual constructionist approaches obviously cover a wide span, from those who appear to assume that, say, official statistics are pretty reasonable estimates of social conditions, to those who believe they are occasionally rough approximators, but not often. This range of positions is reflected in the chapters that make up the substantive core of this volume.

So, what makes a child or young person's account a good one? First, it will bear some relation to our approximate understanding of real social conditions - it will display what Hammersley calls 'subtle realism' (Hammersley, 1992). The position of most contributors in the following chapters is that children and young people's accounts are, in Williamson's words, 'special but not uniquely privileged'. 'Experience' is not its own justification.

> Merely taking experience into account does not reflect on how that experience came to be. In short, oppressive systems are replicated rather than criticised in the unquestioning reliance on 'experience'
>
> (Olesen, 1994: 167)

Second, it will be a plausible account. It will be coherent, and make sense of all the available information. While an account will not usually resolve every puzzle, it will make better sense than other possible narratives, and will do so in ways that are not fraught with obvious contradictions, stupidity and so forth. There are sometimes special difficulties when applying this criterion to children's accounts. Corsaro's observational study of pre-school children aged between two and four years included the use of video evidence to check out whether the children gave comparable interpretations of events he had previously filmed in the setting. He gives examples of extracts from taped interviews with two boys talking about a given episode on film, in which Corsaro tried to use a form of member validation described by Cicourel as 'indefinite triangulation'. His conclusion is that, use of indefinite triangulation with children of this age is a difficult process. Young children seldom reflect on past activities in this fashion, and when asked to do so they often find the task tedious and uninteresting

(Corsaro, 1985: 141).

Ethics

Sociologists' codes of ethics have often failed to give special thought to ethical issues in research involving children. Ethnographers can lay no claim to be exempted from this neglect. Indeed, proponents of qualitative research have on occasion raised their voices in defence of the argument that qualitative research is in some senses more ethical than experimental or survey traditions, on the grounds, for example, that it is less likely to objectify those on whom researchers rely for evidence.

This argument cannot be sustained. The ethical issues created by ethnographic inquiry may find distinctive expression, but they are no less acute. Indeed, it has more recently been acknowledged that ethnography raises especially acute considerations arising from the extent to which it is intrusive in peoples' lives (eg Stacey, 1988). This intrusiveness demands particular sensitivity when children are the subjects of inquiry. The risk of betrayal of trust - to which social workers and teachers are acutely exposed - is of equal importance to researchers. Butler and Williamson, in their portrayal of a child-centred picture of children's worst experiences and deepest anxieties, illustrated also in their chapter in this book, observe the different dimensions of trust. The readiness of some children to say to these relatively passing researchers that they could trust 'someone like you' (Butler and Williamson, 1994: 33) illustrates the problems of easy trust and the potential for ethical abuse that such trust presents. Methods that call on personal experience inevitably raise these questions. 'When we become characters in their stories we change their stories' (Clandinin and Connelly, 1994: 422), which, while it can be positive, carries risk and underlines the need to care for those who share their stories with us.

Fine and Sandstrom offer one of the clearest discussions of ethical issues, and suggest that there are three main areas where such issues arise. These are in the fields of informed consent, the possibility of harm and risk to children, and decisions about how to respond to unpleasant or unacceptable behaviour on the part of children and young people.

We have already pin-pointed one aspect of the problem of *informed consent* in talking about the dangers of easy trust. Indeed, *adult* consent to undertake work with children is often more time consuming and difficult to negotiate. The understandable warnings from schools about 'stranger danger' add to this difficulty. Also, despite the best efforts of researchers, it is likely that younger children in particular will fit the researcher into their world however clear the explanation given (cf Corsaro, 1985). A further complication may arise from considerations of confidentiality. Children and young people may have different views from adults and *want* to be named! In their discussion of children's rights in AIDS research, Rotheram and Koopman point out that ethnographic research raises ethical tension between confidentiality and clinical concerns very acutely, because ethnographers are more likely to witness unacceptable or risky behaviour. In these circumstances 'the researcher needs both morality and strategy; the first without the second is ineffectual; the second without the first is cruel' (1992: 160). When it comes to occasions where the young person refuses to participate, it is our view that there are no special circumstances. The right to refuse is as strong for the child as for the adult and should be given similar weight.

What is the responsibility of adult researchers in potentially harmful situations? Aggression, mischief and cruelty are examples from everyday experience. Ethical concerns arise more frequently in participant observation research. Adults in the vicinity of the research will act as if the researcher is caring for their interests even when the researcher does not believe that is part of the research bargain. Mandell (1988) reports one incident when she found herself watching and not intervening when a risk of moderate harm was evident. More commonly, participant observers are likely to find themselves involved in some level of 'reactive policing' when called on to intervene by one child against another.

The balance is difficult to strike. Disclosure of physical, emotional or sexual harm needs anticipatory planning, so that researchers do not respond without thought when it happens. Special issues arise in some of the participant research carried out in youth gangs or networks, though they fall largely outside the span of research reported in this volume. The usual approach of adopting a gang role that allows non-involvement in overtly unethical or criminal behaviour is not without its moral tensions (Polsky, 1971; Parker, 1974; Williamson, 1981: 516-520).

Harm to the child shades over into more general instances of unpleasant or unacceptable behaviour. Fine and Sandstrom believe that

> Children must be permitted to engage in certain actions and speak certain words that the adult researcher finds distressing. Further, in some instances, the researcher must

act in ways that are at least tacitly supportive of these distressing behaviours

(Fine and Sandstrom, 1988: 55).

Take as examples the occurrence of racist or sexist talk, or minor theft. The natural tendency of sensitive and aware researchers, along with social workers or teachers, may be to *challenge* the former and seek to *understand* the latter. But they also need to observe and try to understand the former, while not responding in ways that make sexist or racist talk more salient than it otherwise would be. The wider issue of the possible sexual dimension of relations between researchers and informants has been neglected and requires discussion (cf Bloor and McKeganey, 1989).

In general, it is important that the researcher first listen to the story, and that it is the informant who tells the story. This requires the 'mutual construction of the research relationship in which both (informants) and researchers feel cared for and a voice with which to tell their stories' (Connelly and Clandinin, 1990: 4). Researchers are not there to conduct 'a raid on mislaid identities' (the phrase is Dannie Abse's from his poem, *Return to Cardiff*).

Methods of inquiry

We observed earlier that strongly held beliefs about childhood as an unfolding of developmental stages has constrained the methods of many researchers, and led to a model of child interviewing which it is believed 'can help the clinician assess the developmental sophistication of the child's interpersonal style and social-emotional reasoning' (Bierman and Schwartz, 1986: 276). However, interviewing strategies in research with children and young people have developed from this position in two directions. *First*, there has been a welcome and quite widespread acceptance of children as persons who have similar rights to those of adults in regard to giving informed consent to research access.

Most of the chapters in this book start from this very premise. For example, Butler and Williamson, in work reported here and elsewhere, gave children the choice as to how they wished to be interviewed - whether singly, in pairs or in groups. They had warm-up sessions with children and young people to convey this ethos and freedom to pursue a particular line of thought. They put them in control of both the tape recorder and the length of interview. When conducting an individual interview they accepted that it 'does not lend itself to tight structures and defined sequences. Children jump around and researchers have to jump with them' (Butler and Williamson, 1994: 30). This often included responding to children's humour and recognising the importance children seemed to attach to researchers conveying 'serious listening inside a funny shell' (p46).

The *second* development in interviewing with children and young people is, if anything, more far reaching. At its heart it involves a major reversal of how we view the interview, so that it is seen not as a source of information from young informants, but as data in and of itself. For instance, talking to adolescents is not a means of gaining information about socialisation processes but, from this perspective, is itself an instance of socialisation. Baker's 'second look' at interviews with adolescents exemplifies this approach. She argues that 'the key to turning the interview into a resource is to view it as a real event in the real world - not only as a means of access to data but as data' (Baker, 1983: 501, 508). This allows her to see the way the interviews display their character as adult-young person social encounters in which adults are questioning adolescents. The questions contain an implicit adult theory of adolescence and answers contain an implicit adolescent theory of adulthood. Interviews are an occasion for the management of identity.

Much of this analysis has come to depend on the proliferation of technology in analysing text. Corsaro and Streeck warned some time ago of the implications of the researcher's greatly expanded information processing capacity, which becomes much greater than that of the individual who is talking. 'The problem is especially acute when studying young children because researchers naturally tend to interpret the data from an adult rather than a child perspective' (1986: 28). But this does not lessen the persuasiveness of Baker's analysis. 'Interviews are socialisation sites. In these interviews adolescents are invited to show membership in the adult language community by making sense of the questions and developing the discourse with the interviewer' (pp 516-517).

Siegert has drawn similar conclusions from his analysis of the paradox of seeking to measure children's competences through interviews. Data from such interviews give insight into competences displayed by children when they interact with adults. Interviews with young children are often conducted in educational settings, where children assume that adult questions have an adult right answer. The paradox of such research is that children are asked to give information about behaviour that occurred in an *egalitarian* context, in a setting which itself is highly *asymmetrical*. He concludes that 'data from interviews which are conducted by an adult interviewer give us more insight into competences displayed by children in interaction with adults ... It is questionable, however, if these findings can be generalised to other contexts, especially to contexts of peer interaction' (Siegert, 1986: 373). Conclusions of this kind clearly have implications beyond the research encounter, and also are relevant to problem solving talk between adults and children in health, social work and educational settings.

Siegert suggests that peer relations may be better investigated through participant observation and group discussions. The extent to which participant observation is possible for adults researching children is an important area of continuing debate, and one where the central problem concerns the membership role adopted by the researcher. This may range from the detached observer, not unlike the use of observation facilities in clinical and therapeutic practice, through the reactive, 'special friend' adopted by Corsaro in his excellent study of children in a nursery school (1985), to the 'responsive, interactive, fully involved participant observer role with the children, in as least an adult role as possible', practised and advocated by Mandell (1988). She presses the advantages of taking a role which minimises social distance, suspends judgements on children's immaturities, engages in joint action with children, and risks being taken for a fool. Her position has been criticised (eg by Fine and Sandstrom) on the grounds that it is not possible to 'bracket' adult/child differences during research. The underlying issue is whether qualitative research with children is in essence different from similar research with adults. Mandell is ready to 'apply adult-adult research strategies to adult-child studies' (p436). In either case the researcher engages in a reflective activity which distinguishes participant observation with children from that with adults, in that they may mine their own experience. This 'differentiates this type of participant observation from most others in which we have never experienced the emotions, social position, or even some of the culture of the group being studied' (Fine and Sandstrom, 1988: 76).

Focus groups offer an alternative method of qualitative inquiry which can and should be further developed with children (Morgan, 1988; Morgan, 1993; Kreuger, 1994). A variant of focus group is illustrated by Bond's account of a day's programme for three ten year old short term foster girls, in which their views were being sought about a family centre. A group discussion format was set up. Dressing up, food, paint, cooking, poster preparation, photography and a presentation were used in an innovative attempt to learn service user views from children (Bond, 1990-1991). However, the application of focus groups methods to social work and research on children has thus far been very limited (Shaw, 1996). The work reported by Katz in this volume offers an important extension of this research.

Personal texts also offer special opportunities for understanding with children and young people. For example, journals provide a way of giving accounts of experience. Children and adolescents often keep journals of their thoughts, activities and stories. Most of these remain private, and it is usually only the accident of history that brings to public view the childhood writings of an Anna Frank or the Bronte children. Childhood memories of those who come within the sphere of influence of social workers are more often emotions recollected in the relative tranquillity of older years (eg Courtney, 1989). But it is likely that some children and young people with whom practitioners work keep journals as attempts to make sense of their experiences - 'capturing fragments of experience in attempts to sort themselves out' (Clandinin and Connelly, 1994: 421). Adults speaking of their experiences as a child do, of course, raise special difficulties for the hearer. Who is speaking?

> Is it the adult interpreting the childhood experience, in which case it is the adult speaking. Or is it the adult expressing the child's story as the child would have told the experience, in which case it is the child speaking (p424).

Recent developments in the field of life histories and life course sociology also prompt researchers to innovative methods of qualitative inquiry with children and young people, as in Burchardt's account of step-children's memories (1990), and Bowen's (1993) application of life history methods to understanding and working with school non-attenders.

The 'practical' implications of engaging in qualitative inquiry cannot be sidestepped (Shaw, 1996). The value of an empirical grasp of kids' culture, the transformation of traditional methods of professional investigation, and the radical implications of understanding for and with children, extend far beyond discipline boundaries. The clearest evidence for this can be found in the subsequent chapters.

Do we need a special qualitative sociology of childhood? This is not, perhaps, the best way to present the question. Rather, just as for John Milton 'New presbyter is but old priest writ large', so for the qualitative inquirer for and with children, the demands, challenges and opportunities of research are those of general qualitative sociology spotlighted, accentuated and 'writ large'.

References

Altheide, D. and Johnson, J. (1994), 'Criteria for Assessing Interpretive Validity in Qualitative Research' in Denzin, N. and Lincoln, Y. (eds) *Handbook of Qualitative Research*, Newbury Park, Sage.

Baker, C. (1983). 'A Second Look at Interviews with Adolescents' in *Journal of Youth and Adolescence*, Vol. 12, No. 6.

Best, J. (1987), 'Rhetoric in Claims Making' in *Social Problems* Vol. 34, No. 2.

Best, J. (ed) (1989), *Images of Issues: Typifying Contemporary Social Problems*, New York, Aldine de Gruyter.

Bierman, K. and Schwartz, L. (1986), 'Clinical Child Interviews: Approaches and development Considerations' in *Child and Adolescent Psychotherapy*, Vol. 3, No. 4.

Bloor, M. and McKeganey, N. (1989), 'Ethnography Addressing the Practitioner' in Gubrium, J. and Silverman, D. (eds) *The Politics of Field Research: Sociology Beyond Enlightenment*, Newbury Park, Sage.

Bond, M. (1990-1991), '"The Centre, It's for Children': Seeking Children's Views as Users of a Family Centre' in *Practice*, Vol. 7, No. 1.

Bowen, D. (1993), 'The Delights of Learning To Apply The Life History Method To School Non-attenders' In Broad, B and Fletcher, C (eds) *Practitioner Research*, London, Whiting and Birch.

Bowles, S. and Gintis, H. (1976), *Schooling in Capitalist America*, London, Routledge and Kegan Paul.

Brannen, J. and O'Brian, M. (1995), 'Childhood and the Sociological Gaze: Paradigms and Paradoxes' in *Sociology* Vol.29, No.4.

Burchardt, N. (1990), 'Stepchildren's Memories: Myth, Understanding and Forgiveness' in Samuel, R. and Thompson, P. *The Myths we Live By*, London, Routledge.

Butler, I. and Williamson, H. (1994), *Children Speak: Children, Trauma and Social Work*, London, Longman.

Cicourel, A., Jennings, K., Leiter, K., MacKay, E., Mehan, H. and Roth, D. (1974), *Language Use and Schools Performance*, New York, Academic Press.

Clandinin, D. and Connelly, F. (1994), 'Personal Experience Methods' in Denzin, N. and Lincoln, Y. (eds) *Handbook of Qualitative Research*, Newbury Park, Sage.

Connelly, F. and Clandinin, D. (1990), 'Stories of Experience and Narrative Inquiry' in *Educational Researcher*, Vol. 19, No. 5.

Corsaro, W. (1985), *Friendship and Peer Culture in the Early Years*, New Jersey, Ablex, Norwood.

Corsaro, W. and Streeck, J. (1986), 'Studying Children's Worlds: Methodological Issues' in Cook-Gumperz, J., Corsaro, W. and Streeck, J. (eds) *Children's Worlds and Children's Language*, Berlin, Mouton de Gruyter.

Courtney, C. (1989), *Morphine and Dolly Mixtures*, Cardiff, Honno.

Denzin, N. (1977), *Childhood Socialisation*, San Francisco, Jossey Bass.

Fine, G. and Sandstrom, K. (1988), *Knowing Children: Participant Observation with Minors*, Newbury Park, Sage.

Goode, D. (1986), 'Kids, Culture and Innocents' in *Human Studies*, Vol. 9, No. 1.

Hammersley, P. (1992), *What's Wrong With Ethnography?*, London, Routledge.

Hernandez, D. (1995), *America's Children: Resources From Family, Government and the Economy*. New York, Sage Foundation.

Jenks, C. (ed) (1992), *The Sociology of Childhood*, Aldershot, Gregg Revivals.

Kreuger, R. (ed) (1994), *Focus Groups: a Practical Guide for Applied Research*, Newbury Park, Sage.

Mandell, N. (1988), 'The Least Adult Role in Studying Children' in *Journal of Contemporary Ethnography*, Vol. 16, No. 4.

Mayall, B. (ed) (1994), *Children's Childhoods: Observed and Experienced*. London, Falmer Press.

Morgan, D. L. (1988), *Focus groups as Qualitative Research*, Newbury Park, Sage.

Morgan, D. L. (ed) (1993), *Successful Focus groups: Advancing the State of the Art*, Newbury Park, Sage.

Olesen, V. (1994), 'Feminisms and Models of Qualitative Research' in Denzin, N. and Lincoln, Y. (eds) *Handbook of Qualitative Research*, Newbury Park, Sage.

Opie, I. and Opie, P. (1959), *The Lore and Language of Schoolchildren*, Oxford, Oxford University Press.

Opie, I. and Opie, P. (1969), *Children's Games of Street and Playground*, Oxford, Oxford University Press.

Opie, I. and Opie, P. (1991), 'The Culture of Children', in Waksler, F. (ed), *Studying the Social Worlds of Children: Sociological Readings*, Farnborough, Saxon House.

Parker, H. (1974), *View From the Boys*, David and Charles, Newton Abbott.

Parker, W. (1984), 'Interviewing Children: Problems and Promise' in *Journal of Negro Education*, Vol. 53, No. 1.

Pilcher, J. (1995), *Age and Generation*, Oxford, Oxford University Press.

Polsky, N. (1971), *Hustlers, Beats and Others*. Harmondsworth, Penguin.

Qvortrup, J. (1990), 'A Voice for Children in Statistical and Social Accounting: A Plea for Children's Right to be Heard', in James, A. and Prout, A. (eds) *Constructing and Reconstructing Childhood: Contemporary Issues in the Sociological Study of Childhood'*, Basingstoke: Falmer.

Qvortrup, J., Bardy, M., Sgritta, G. and Wintersberger, H. (1994), (eds), *Childhood Matters: Social Theory, Practice and Politics*, Aldershot, Avebury.

Rotheram, M. and Koopman, C. (1992), 'Protecting Children's Rights in AIDS Research' in Stanley, B. and Sieber, J. (eds) *Social Research on Children and Adolescents: Ethical Issues*, Newbury Park, Sage.

Saporitti, A. (1994), 'A Methodology for Making Children Count', in Qvortrup, J., Bardy, M., Sgritta, G. and Wintersberger, H. (eds), *Childhood Matters: Social Theory, Practice and Politics*, Aldershot, Avebury.

Shaw, I. (1996), *Evaluating in Practice*, Aldershot: Ashgate.

Siegert, M. (1986), 'Adult Elicited Child Behaviour: The Paradox of Measuring Social Competence Through Interviewing' in Cook-Gumperz, J., Corsaro, W. and Streeck, J. (eds) *Children's Worlds and Children's Language*, Berlin: Mouton de Gruyter.

Stacey, J. (1988), 'Can There be a Feminist Ethnography?' in *Women's Studies International*, Vol. 11, No. 1.

Waksler, F. C. W. (ed) (1991), *Studying the Social Worlds of Children: Sociological Readings*, Farnborough, Saxon House.

Williamson, H. (1981), *Juvenile Justice and Working Class Community*, Unpublished PhD Thesis, University of Wales.

Willis, P. (1978), *Learning to Labour*, Farnborough, Saxon House.

3 'Mirror, mirror on the wall. Who is the fairest of them all?' Involuntary childlessness and identity

Julie Selwyn

The birth of a child is a time of celebration; a celebration not only of a new life but of a change in status for parents. A child links the generations and provides continuity between the past, present and future. Why is it so important to have children? Societal expectations are that couples in a long term heterosexual relationship will have a child. There are some groups of adults, for example gay and lesbian couples, who are not encouraged to have children and other adults who choose to remain childless. Their experiences can tell us much about the significance of children for adults (Veevers, 1980; Bozett, 1987). However, for the purposes of this chapter the discussion will concentrate on heterosexual couples who want children. In this chapter I will attempt to explain the symbolic importance of children for adults. To begin this exploration the question of children's importance is looked at from a different perspective. Some couples are unable to have children due to fertility problems. This group of people want to fulfil their own and society's expectations, but are unable to do so. What are their experiences of the social and psychological pressures faced in a pronatalist society? The literature is reviewed and is followed by an account of how ten infertile couples attempted to find a solution to their childlessness by trying to adopt. All were unsuccessful and other solutions were sought in their determination to have a child. For these couples the desire for a child was so strong that it took precedence over every area of their lives.

There are no positive images of childlessness in our society for heterosexual couples. Cultural evaluations of fertility are reflected in language - pregnant with hope, a barren land, a sterile environment. Although infertility is not a disease, medical terminology uses similar moral imagery - a hostile vagina, blighted ovum, incompetent spermatozoa. Popular stereotypes of the childless conjure up images of women as either pathetic and sad, doting in an eccentric or obsessive way on animals or as emotionless career women. Men may be seen as secret homosexuals or as insensitive and hard nosed. Couples may be thought of as being self absorbed, prioritising the acquisition of wealth and material goods (Houghton and Houghton, 1987). Unlike many other stigmas which have either changed over time (e.g. epilepsy), or been turned by some people into a source of pride (e.g. homosexuality), childlessness has always been viewed negatively. Fairy stories portray the childless as dangerous, evil and ugly. In Snow White the queen challenges her reflection in the mirror to confirm the view she has of herself. Interestingly, most illustrations show a woman who is vain, proud and overbearing. She is so self absorbed that it is implicit that she must be childless. Witches try to tempt children away from their parents and take them as their own. There is a struggle between the crafty, evil witch and the innocence and intelligence of children. Folk tales illustrate that childlessness has a long tradition of being viewed negatively and carries an ancient social stigma (Burgwyn, 1981).

Hidden childlessness

Infertility is an area that has received little attention in feminist, anthropological or sociological literature. Interest has been focused on the development of the new medical technologies, eg in-vitro fertilisation (IVF), or on those women who choose a child free lifestyle (Veevers, 1980). From the 1930's governments have shied away from supporting research that asks intimate questions of couples' sexual behaviour. A plea for accurate data was a recommendation of the Warnock Committee on Human Fertilisation and Embryology (Warnock, 1985) as so little was known of the numbers affected by childlessness. This was ignored by a Conservative Government which was ideologically opposed to research that would ask intimate questions about family life and sexual behaviour. The available data is taken from demographic statistics and research samples drawn from people attending fertility clinics. These have their limitations. Primary infertility is defined as a failure to conceive after one year of intercourse without contraception and if there has been no live birth before. Secondary infertility however, is a failure to conceive after one or more births, or following conception, a failure to carry a pregnancy to full term (McFalls, 1979). Demographic statistics give no indication of the extent of primary or secondary infertility, nor whether the childlessness is voluntary or involuntary.

A large part of research on fertility has been of a statistical nature, involving attempts to distinguish those aspects of development (as represented by socio-economic indices of various sorts) that are most closely related to infertility. Such research often has been undertaken to determine the origins of fertility declines in the past or to account for regional differences in fertility. Statistical techniques employed have ranged from two or three dimensional cross tabulations to path analysis and multi-regression techniques, whilst the data have been collected from individuals by survey and from regions and countries by collating information from a number of sources. However, despite thirty five years of research there is an absence of an accepted theory of fertility change. Fertility decline started around 1965 and took governments by surprise (Davis, 1986). Theories suggest that fertility is affected by the relationship between the economic costs and benefits that childbearing entails (Coale, 1973), or by social pressures (McNicoll, 1975), or the various Marxist approaches (Hollander, 1984) where the main emphasis is on the survival strategies employed by families to cope with capitalist structures.

European countries have reached levels of fertility that twenty years ago would have been considered unbelievable (Davis *et al*, 1986). Demographic statistics show the birth rate is falling in all European countries with the present birth rate in the United Kingdom ten per cent below the replacement rate needed to balance the population (Coleman, 1993). Is infertility increasing? Current forecasts (Bhrolchain, 1993) suggest that as many as seventeen per cent of women born in England and Wales after 1975 will remain childless. This is in contrast with fertility surveys which suggest about five per cent of women want to remain childless (EC Commission, 1990). However, it is known that peoples' wishes change over time. Some observers like Irvine (1994) state that sperm counts are dropping by two per cent each year and have reduced fifty per cent since the war. Dutch research (Carlsen *et al*, 1992) suggests that environmental pollution is the main cause of reduced fertility. Others claim it only *appears* that infertility is increasing as the new technologies bring people out for treatment and women choose to delay childbearing until their late thirties. The belief that infertility is increasing taps into deep seated fears. Children are a visible link to the future and represent continuity and security. Childlessness threatens the sense of order, both in a biological and a sociological sense. At a time when national and international boundaries and institutions are challenged, the sense of order is threatened. The millennium also seems to raise fears about the future. P.D. James in her best selling novel *Children of Men* (1994) explores these fears, developing a plot where sometime in the near future all men are infertile and the last generation is on earth. Margaret Atwood's novels have drawn on similar ideas (e.g. *The Handmaid's Tale*). These deep-seated fears arise because Western medicine and science have failed to find the cause or a solution. This is not a new phenomenon as there were similar concerns about infertility increasing at the start of this century (Pfeffer, 1994).

The data available on the number of couples affected by involuntary childlessness are unreliable and impressionistic. Data are available from studies of couples who attend fertility clinics. These have been generally conducted by clinicians whose main area of interest is new medical technologies, or because of an interest in links between psychiatric illness and infertility. Samples from clinics tend to be small, American in origin, and consist of interviews with women. Men have been excluded as respondents as, it is claimed, they deter the female partner from answering questions, they are unreliable and often unavailable for interview (see Miall 1986, and Population Investigation Committee archives as examples) The views of minority ethnic communities are also missing. The typical respondent is a white, female, middle class American. There is very little British research. Many areas of Britain do not have fertility treatment available on the National Health Service. It is a private service for those who can afford to pay. Samples therefore exclude those on low incomes. There are no data on how people from different socio-economic groups respond to a diagnosis of infertility. Social and social-psychological aspects of infertility have been ignored.

Hull's study (1985) of a single health district (Bristol) suggests that one in six couples needs medical help to conceive. Although this study is often quoted, there are dangers in assuming the same will apply in all health districts. Other estimates put the figure at between one in four and one in ten (Burgwyn, 1981; Mosher, 1982) of the population. However, a retrospective study (Templeton et al, 1990) found that one in three women in Aberdeen who were past the childbearing years had not consulted a doctor about their difficulty in conceiving. They had never seen their GP or visited a fertility clinic. Present knowledge of the extent of infertility and whether it is increasing or decreasing is limited. However, there are a significant number of people affected by involuntary childlessness and as Philipp (1983) notes:

> There are at least one million couples in the United Kingdom who are at this moment wishing for a baby, or pregnancy and have been trying for years to achieve their desire.

Gender differences

The stigma of infertility seems to be present in most cultures. Hindu women in Northern India who fail to conceive within two years of marriage can be returned to their father's home. Alive or dead, childless women possess an 'evil eye' and are frequently blamed for fires and for attempted abductions of children. All kinds of protective measures are taken to prevent this from happening particularly around the time of birth (Kolenda, 1982). Childless women are also viewed as dangerous in Western culture. Warner (1993) states that childbearing became the raison d'être of women; the only excuse for female seductiveness and desirability. Women are tamed and rendered safe by childbirth.

A theme develops that takes the infertile woman who has passed the age of childbearing as representing in some fundamental way a transgression against the purpose of her sex and in that transgression against the natural God-given order. She can then serve to represent other pejorative and repulsive or repugnant aberrations. Hence the connection between beauty and virtue, ugliness and vice. And one has to remember that this still persists as a very pernicious aspect of our combined moral and aesthetic judgements (Warner 1993).

The negative impact of infertility also comes from what Goffman (1963) termed 'spoiled identity'. In the only available work that focuses on identity and infertility Miall (1986) examined the reactions of women to their own and their husband's infertility. She took as her starting point Veevers' (1972) concept of childlessness as a form of deviance in marriage - a violation of prevailing norms of acceptable conduct. Miall explored how far the women viewed their infertility as stigmatising. Nearly all the respondents viewed infertility in a negative light representing some form of failure. Interestingly, over sixty per cent of women who were infertile and fifty per cent of the women who were married to an infertile man viewed male infertility as more stigmatising than female infertility. More than half hesitated to tell others and seventy-five per cent engaged in some form of information management.

There is dispute in the literature about which gender is the most seriously affected by a diagnosis of infertility. Burnage (1977) and Humphrey (1969) argue that men are the more seriously affected. They note that it is only men who regard infertility as linked with sexual performance and there has long been a popular correlation of fertility and virility (from the Latin vir = to be a man). Person (1980) argues that in men, gender appears to 'lean on' sexuality because the need for sexual performance is so great. In women, gender identity and self worth can be consolidated by other means. As men become more involved in child care their expectations are changing. Men are beginning to look to parenthood to provide the personal fulfilment that traditionally was found through work. The impact of male unemployment and changing work patterns for men and women have all placed greater emphasis on the role of the father (Butterworth 1994).

In contrast it has been argued that the long standing cultural motherhood mandate (Russo, 1976; Sandelowski, 1990) means that women bear the brunt of infertility. Patriarchal traditions, the unequal status of women and men in heterosexual relationships, and the passing of property down the male line, historically have defined infertility as a female problem. Women bear the social onus for childlessness (Higgins, 1990) and the search for available alternatives (Kandiyoti, 1988). Medical investigations and treatment are primarily focused on the woman's body, irrespective of which partner is infertile. Without her partner's agreement, the woman cannot obtain his sperm for insemination or consent to IVF, nor choose adoption or donor insemination. Lorber and Bandlamundi (1993) note how a bargaining relationship develops. Women take on the burden of infertility changing the definition to 'our infertility'.

Spoiled identities

Preparation for adult life presumes there will be children. Glick (1977) reports that ninety-five per cent of newly married couples want and expect to have children. As the Le Masters (1957) study showed parenthood, not marriage, is the real romantic complex in our society. Berger and Kellner (1970) stated that marriage is a process of redefinition where two strangers come together and redefine themselves. They emphasise that this process is aided by others external to the relationship who assist in co-defining the new reality. Childlessness involves a major reconstruction of reality by partners, family and friends. Berger and Kellner (1970) also suggested that a primary function of marriage is to provide a couple with a distinctive private world over which they have some control and can shape, in contrast with the outside world over which they have little control. Matthews and Matthews (1986) conclude that

> Infertility not only calls into question the biological function of marriage related to the procreation of children but it also directly challenges the social function of marriage as providing some control over a private world.

> (p.643)

Instead of marriage providing the couple with the sort of order in which they can experience life as making sense (Berger and Kellner, 1970), childless couples are gradually confronted with a situation of which they can make no sense. Lerner (1980) states people need to believe in a just world; a world which is a stable and orderly, a place where people get what they deserve. This leads infertile couples to search their own and each others' personal histories looking for some guilty deed that might explain their childlessness. Childlessness also helps others to distance themselves from infertility believing it couldn't happen to them. Couples who have married only to find they are infertile are denied access to a fundamental rite of passage. Following Glaser and Strauss' (1986) work on status passages, childlessness can be seen as an involuntary, undesirable and frequently irreversible status passage.

Mahlstedt (1980) identifies eight areas of loss involved with infertility. There are losses of relationship (both real and imagined), health, status, self-esteem, confidence, security and hope. Houghton and Houghton (1987) try to define what it is that makes the prospect of life without children so fearful. They describe three fears: the thwarting of love, peripherality and genetic death. The childless face difficulties in experiencing some of the love relationships that are normally taken for granted. They are deprived of the parent/child relationship, deprived of the dreams and aspirations that adults have for their children, and their own social networks constrict as friendships decrease. Where adoption is not possible, there is no-one who wants the love they have to give, and as a result couples can become absorbed with each other. Occupations such as social work and nursing, which in the past might have provided childless people with opportunities to experience some elements of parenting have restricted this part of the role. Experiencing other types of relationship with a child, for example being a godparent, may not give the childless the commitment they seek, and they may feel peripheral to extended family decisions and day to day life.

Genetic death refers to a role given to people who are not contributing to the future of the human race. There is a common thread in the literature around the need of humans to find a meaning or purpose in their lives. For some, religious beliefs provide an answer but for others a child satisfies this need. Hoffman et al (1976) argue that in highly industrialised societies where people are more distant from basic life processes (the earth, birth, death) the need for something that ties them to the future is important. Hoffman and Hoffman (1976) state that having children is a way of reproducing oneself and having one's own characteristics and beliefs reflected in another who will live on after one is dead is another way of achieving a kind of immortality.

Children are a tie to the past, carrying the genes of ancestors, traditions and memories. They are also a tie to the future as they will carry these onto the next generation. They provide the present life with a meaning. In a secular society, children represent achievement and creativity.

Stigma

The stigma of infertility can be divided across the six dimensions identified by Jones (1984). First, *concealability;* how easily is the discreditable attribute hidden? Infertility is not immediately obvious, but in any social discourse becomes so. Social conversations, particular those where people are meeting for the first time, often include enquiries about number and ages of children. Those who are childless are readily identified. Secondly, the *course;* does the stigma change over time? The outcome for those who are infertile is varied. Some, (Keeble, 1994 estimates only eighteen per cent) will be helped by medical technology, while others will try a range of other solutions for example adoption or surrogacy. For the majority of involuntary childless couples, childlessness will continue to be experienced as a stigma throughout their lives. Infertility has become increasingly medicalised. Becker and Nachtingall (1994) argue that as the medical profession now dominates the infertility area, the range of solutions for infertility has decreased. Instead of infertility being seen as a social problem with several possible solutions, it is seen as a medical one, with only one solution - the birth of a child. Couples where treatment is unsuccessful experience a dual failure. Not only is there a failure to achieve a successful pregnancy but they have also failed to respond to medical treatment. Thirdly, *disruptiveness;* how far does the stigma disrupt relationships? The childless find their networks narrow as peers have children and similar interests are no longer shared. Houghton and Houghton (1977) note how the childless find themselves excluded from previously close relationships once children are born and excluded from family occasions. Fourthly, *origin;* how did the discreditable attribute come about? Childless people question who is at fault and who is to blame. This often leads to a review of each others lives, looking for perhaps some sexual indiscretion or some guilty deed on which to hang the blame. Fifthly, *peril;* how much of a threat does the stigma represent to society? The childless pose a threat to shared meanings of the world. Societies are, of necessity, pronatalist, in that parenthood is normative in all societies. If a society is to continue each generation must recruit the next generation to spend a high proportion of their lives caring for children. Finally, *aesthetic qualities;* childlessness is seen as unattractive and an aspect of the stigmatising process is that personality and physical characteristics are assumed to be unattractive too. Infertility renders the involuntary childless 'less than whole' people (Veevers, 1980).

Stigma can only be understood in terms of large scale historical, cultural and social forces (Stafford and Stafford, 1986). The stigma of infertility appears to be changing; the medicalisation of infertility, the changing role of men, the importance of children in providing a meaning for adult lives, the expectation that children will provide emotional fulfilment for adults, coupled with a highly industrialised society, reflect the increasing psychological value of children for adults. However there is a small group of women who have chosen childlessness and their views on stigma are interesting. Veevers' (1980) sample of 156 voluntarily childless women were aware of societal expectations and experienced angry confrontations with many people who thought their choice was immoral. However over time the majority became more and more adept at dealing with enquiries about their lack of children and accepted they would always be viewed as a little odd by others. The benefits of a child-free life style or their dislike of children far outweighed any concerns about negative reactions. Those who are childless by choice (Smith, 1995) are becoming more vocal, defending their right not to have a child. Their impact on the stigma of childlessness has been minimal but may, if more women make this choice, begin to disturb the long-standing negative view of childlessness.

The study

My interest in this area was originally sparked by working with couples applying to adopt and observing the impact of infertility. All who applied to adopt thought they would make good adoptive parents. Some applicants were turned down and were unable to adopt. The research study set out to examine the experiences and perceptions of infertile couples who had been rejected by an adoption agency and to discover if they had found other solutions to their childlessness. These couples are perhaps the ones who feel the desire for a child most strongly. Not only have they had years of unsuccessful fertility treatment but they then go through the adoption process to try and achieve their desire for a child. The first difficulty was in finding a sample. Several adoption agencies refused requests for access to couples who had been turned down, stating the subject matter was too sensitive for investigation. One adoption agency did agree and thirty-six couples were contacted who had been turned down between 1980-1986. Ten couples agreed to participate in interviews lasting in total length between three to five hours. The sensitive nature of the topic, changes in marital status and residence and the request to interview both partners reduced the number of respondents. The number of respondents cannot be taken as representative. The purpose of the qualitative interview is not to discover how many and what kinds of people share certain characteristics, views and assumptions but to examine the views and assumptions themselves. Hakim (1987) comments on how qualitative research offers information on the way attitudes and experiences cohere into meaningful patterns and offers substantively different and complimentary information to quantitative methods. Although non probability sampling has some limitations it provides a way of exploring areas where little is known. What was needed was a piece of exploratory research, giving the respondents a chance to tell their story in their own way. To do this, I chose the idiom of the long interview as,

> The method can take us into the mental world of the interviewee, to glimpse the categories and logic by which he or she sees the world. It can also take us into the lifeworld of the individual to see the context, and pattern of daily experience.

> (McCracken, 1988 p.9)

The respondents had wanted children for varying lengths of time. Five of the ten couples dated this from the time of their marriage - '...it was one reason why we got married'. Others could not remember a time when they did not want children. Four women were infertile, two men, one unexplained infertility, one couple where both partners were infertile, and two couples who had been advised for medical reasons not to have any more children. The last two couples had a child but stated they felt the need for another child strongly. The pain was described as 'magnified'. Their one child was a visible reminder of something they could not replicate. For all the respondents an absent child dominated their lives.

Eight couples had undergone fertility treatment, lasting anything between four and fourteen years. The average length was seven years. The low success rate, high cost physically, emotionally and financially were all seen as difficult characteristics of a long slow process. At the time IVF was costing in the region of £1,000 a treatment and there were additional costs such as taking time off work and travelling to hospital. Several couples had taken out second mortgages on their properties and were under severe financial strain. The one positive feature of the whole process that couples cited was their relationship with their consultant. This was the first time any of them could identify someone who really seemed to understand their need for a child. However, when treatment was unsuccessful couples talked about their sense of failure - 'We couldn't get anything right'.

Although the literature suggests that infertile couples are secretive about their infertility, this was not the case for most of these respondents. Seven of the couples told anyone who asked. All these couples thought it was very important that no-one should think they had made a deliberate choice not to have children. They did not want to be thought of as selfish and viewed voluntary childlessness as carrying a greater stigma than involuntary childlessness. The medical diagnosis, although often identifying one of the partners as having an infertility problem, was a confirmation that it was a physical difficulty. This relieved any doubts that it was an emotional problem. All were surprised by the reaction of family and friends. Comments included 'you're trying too hard'; and 'don't worry you're only young ... children are nothing but a burden'.

One man in the sample was infertile (although a further two had been sterilised during previous marriages). He found the comments and jibes distressing. He had confided in his manager at work, who had passed the information on until everyone at his workplace was aware of his 'problem'. He became the target of many cruel jokes, with pornographic material left around for him to find and loud comments about whether he knew how to do 'it' properly. At home his family and friends were visibly disappointed. He was the only son and the family name would die out if he did not provide a son. The family told him often that his infertility did not make him 'less of a man', but he came to believe they meant the opposite as this was repeated so frequently. The three couples who did not reveal their infertility stated they were afraid of gossip - 'if I'd told them it would have been like appearing in *The News of the World*'. Those people who were aware of these couples' difficulties expected a rapid 'cure'. There was a belief that the new medical technologies could solve any problem. After many years the respondents too hung onto the hope that one day they might be cured: 'there's always a chance. Doctors never tell you 100 per cent. No, anyway they might find a cure'.

Women described feelings of intense sadness, and tearful outbursts set off by what they thought of as the slightest thing. Both men and women described difficulty watching television; images of children made them tearful. The news of pregnancy of relatives or friends was viewed angrily.

'If I saw a pregnant women walking down the street I wanted to punch her'. Three of the women were not informed if a family member became pregnant - 'I felt excluded from normal life'. Menstruation brought with it the reminder of failure and one wife remarked it was her 'monthly miscarriage', bringing feelings of emptiness and a void in her life. Eight husbands were in complete agreement with their wives' perceptions and feelings around infertility. The men stated they found it harder to show their upset and grief, and described their feelings as a 'sadness', a 'gap in my life' or as a 'disappointment'. It was clear during the interviews that the men were very distressed by their childlessness but did not always have the language to convey their feelings. Men spoke of their anger at single mothers who 'don't deserve to have children', or spoke of life's unfairness when some seemed to have as many children as they wished even when they were not wanted. Men related stories of neighbours' children who in their eyes were deprived of attention and felt it was cruel when they and their wives had so much to offer. Emotions were difficult to control when children were included in social activities or seen playing in the street. Two men had children by previous marriages and their understanding of the impact of infertility was questioned by their wives. 'It was all on me, my husband didn't care ... it was my load'. Arguments occasionally ended in violence. Men admitted hitting walls, doors and one husband stated he had attacked his wife. In one house a smashed door had been left unrepaired as the couple felt it was a symbol of their unhappiness at that time. As infertility treatment continued both couples felt their marriages were 'breaking up', and the husband's response was to find excuses not to come home, staying out late, going to work earlier in the mornings, anything to avoid another scene. The eight couples who did feel they were trying together to solve their childlessness, also found a marked effect on their lives. One couple moved house twice 'to get away from the neighbours' children ... I couldn't bear to hear them through the walls'. Three couples spent much time and energy planning their lives to avoid any contact with children. Shopping trips were planned to take place when the fewest children were likely to be seen. Holiday dates and destinations were all planned around this consideration. Three women worked, and were in female dominated environments where conversation was often around children and babies. During work hours feelings had to be kept under tight control, and evenings were often spent in tears. The remaining seven women had been advised not to work and hoped that by removing the stress of work there was a greater likelihood of achieving a successful pregnancy.

All ten couples decided that fertility treatment was not going to help them and that adoption would be the next solution to their childlessness.

Between one and three years later all the couples were turned down as suitable adoptive parents. Looking back to that time, no-one could understand why their application had not been successful - they all thought they would have made good adoptive parents. Nine couples tried further infertility treatment. Three of these couples went on to have a successful pregnancy. These couples described themselves as having 'a normal family now'. One couple continued with just one child. The failure to be approved by the adoption agency, was an additional blow. Six couples remained childless. Of these, two were actively considering surrogacy, and another couple were thinking of getting a child from another country by any means, 'whatever it takes'.

All those still childless tried to view the future positively:

> We've reached the end ... We can go on holiday and buy nice things. We try to use the situation to our advantage and indulge ourselves. This works ninety-nine per cent of the time, but doesn't make up for not having children ... their value increases ... we appreciate them more ... Before, hope was still there ... It's inescapable ... I want them more. Nobody really understands. Our parents no longer talk about it. They think you're getting on with life, it's over.

There was a general feeling from all the childless couples that they were just going on, sharing joint interests, and coping by avoidance and distraction. This involved filling up time, by starting businesses, carefully planning holidays and shopping trips, and working harder and longer hours. One husband angrily said 'I'm on the scrap heap, the next generation won't be from this household'. Others voiced their anger at the waste. The wasted years, their youth gone, lost in a round of hospital visits, treatments, social work visits. Men spoke of being well practised at hiding their emotions but stated they felt the childlessness deeply. Time was running out for all the couples and there were fears for the future - fear of a lonely old age and the menopause looming ahead. In spite of years of unsuccessful treatment, all hoped for a miracle cure; they would be the lucky ones who would defy medical explanation. Contact with children was avoided by four couples and the others enjoyed their roles as godparents or aunts and uncles. Friendships had decreased as their peers had had families, and now friends were either significantly younger or older. Couples had anticipated an increased level of love, involvement and support from their parents and friends once they had become parents. This was cruelly mirrored by the couples' feelings of abandonment once parenthood was denied. 'I would have been a different person ... a lot happier ... I can't laugh like others. I have to be careful. I'm too emotional and might burst into tears'.

Conclusion

All the couples believed that they should have been approved as adoptive parents. None were secretive about their rejection. For those who now have children, the adoption agency's decision was held up for ridicule. Having a child and parenting confirmed for them that their own beliefs and self image were accurate. The six childless couples when asked in social situations about their lack of children, pointed out they had tried everything. Two couples had kept the letter from the agency turning them down and showed it to anyone querying their childlessness. It was still more important that others should not think they were childless by choice. The stigma of voluntary childlessness was seen as greater than the stigma of rejection by an adoption agency.

Their accounts were rich in detail and the pain of past events was evident. The men were not reluctant to speak, commenting they were pleased someone was listening. All the couples wanted to know if there were others in the same position as themselves. Survey interviews are designed to take on a ritualistic uniformity with ideally the same questions asked and in the same order. The reality was not like this. As O'Brien and McKee (1982) state, 'The talk and interaction that take place in interview settings have their own degree of autonomy; interviews are social constructs as are our readings of them'. A balance had to be struck between letting the respondents talk and ensuring questions were answered. Couples debated their differing recollections and perceptions of events as each question was asked and this process yielded further data (Selwyn, 1991, 1994). The respondents experienced and are continuing to experience social and psychological pressure to conform to societal expectations. Their accounts confirm much of the literature and give a rare glimpse into how this group construes the world. The importance and significance of a child was evident by the high levels of distress and continued attempts to bring a child into the family. The menopause was acknowledged to be the final event which would put an end to their hopes. However, at the time of interview all the couples were several years away from this and may when the time comes change their expectations and hopes. For these adults, life was not complete without a child. Children were expected to provide a confirmation of maturity, give happiness, a sense of a purpose to life and validate sexual identity.

Throughout this chapter I have argued that children carry powerful symbols. Parents expect children to have similar personality traits to their own and resemble them physically. Parents can relive their own childhood, putting perceived wrongs to right or trying to ensure their child achieves what they could not. Children are a mirror to the future, giving a kind of immortality in an insecure world. Given the importance of children to adults, it is not surprising that children have not been allowed to speak for themselves in the literature. The present social construction of childhood is one that makes children totally dependent on adults.

Those who are involuntarily childless are increasingly turning to the medical profession for help. Adoption was once a service supplying infertile couples with a child. It is now a service for children who need parents who can cope with the demands of parenting children with special needs. The new medical technologies have the role of supplying babies to infertile couples. There has been little debate about the rights of children in this medical process. and even fewer safeguards. For example, the debate around IVF donors has been dominated by the perceived need for secrecy to protect the supply of donors. Unlike adoption, where children upon reaching the age of eighteen are able to trace their birth parents, IVF children have no such legal rights. The new genetics also raise many moral questions. Children are the commodities to be bought if a couple is able. The driving force is the demand to provide children for childless couples who are deeply distressed by their inability to have a child. The decrease in fertility and increased life expectancy have turned the age structure of populations upside down. Children are becoming a smaller percentage of the population. As this trend continues how will the status of children be affected? Will children become more valuable and if so how will their rights be protected? Will children become more invisible or will it bring a real increase in children's power? Whatever the future holds, the challenge is whether as adults we can recognise and put aside the symbols we attach to children and begin to develop systems that genuinely give children civil and political rights.

References

Albee, E. (1963), *Who's Afraid of Virginia Wolf,* New York: Atheneum.

Becker, G. and Nachtingall, R. (1992), 'Eager for medicalization: the social production of infertility as a disease', *Sociology of Health and Illness,* Vol. 14, No. 4, pp 457-471.

Berger, P. and Kellner, H. (1970), 'Marriage and the construction of reality' in Dreitzel, H P (Ed.), *Recent Sociology,* No. 2, New York: Macmillan, pp 392-402.

Bhrolchain, M. (Ed.) (1993), *New Perspectives on Fertility in Britain,* London: HMSO.

Bozett, F. (Ed.) (1987), *Gay and Lesbian Parents,* New York: Praeger.

Burgwyn, D. (1981), *Marriage without children,* New York: Harper and Row.

Burnage, A. (1972), 'Effects of infertility', *Adoption and Fostering,* Vol. 88, No. 2, pp. 47-48.

Butterworth, D. (1994), 'Are Fathers Really Necessary to the Family Unit in Early Childhood?', *OMEP, International Journal of Early Childhood,* Vol. 26, No. 1, pp. 1-5.

Carlsen, B., Giwereman, A., Keiding, N. and Skakkeback, N. E. (1992), 'Evidence for decreasing quality of semen during the past 50 years', *British Medical Journal,* Vol. 305, pp 609-13.

Coale, J. (1973), 'The Demographic Transition Reconsidered', *International Population Conference, Liege,* Vol. 1, pp 53-71, IUSSP.

Coleman, D. (1993), 'Britain in Europe; international and regional comparisons of fertility levels and trends', in Bhrolchain, M. (Ed.), (1993),.*New Perspectives on Fertility in Britain,* London: HMSO

Davis, K., Bernstain, M., Ricardo-Campbell, R. (Ed.) (1986), *Population and Development Review - Below Replacement Fertility in Industrial Societies. Causes, Consequences, Policies,* Cambridge: Cambridge University Press.

EC Commission (1990), *European public opinion on the family and the desire to have children,* Luxembourg: Office for Official Publications of the European Community.

Gibson, C. (1980), 'Childlessness and marital instability. A re-examination of the evidence', *Journal of Bio- social Science,* Vol. 12, No. 2.

Glaser, B. G. and Strauss, A. L. (1986), *Status Passage: A formal theory.* Chicago: Aldine-Atherton.

Glick, P. C. (1977), 'Updating the life-cycle of the family', *Journal of Marriage and the Family,* Vol. 39.

Goffman, E. (1963), *Stigma: Notes on the management of spoiled identities*, Englewood Cliffs, New Jersey: Prentice Hall.

Hakim, C. (1987), *Research Design*, London: Allen and Unwin.

Higgins, B. S. (1990), 'Couple infertility: From the perspective of the close relationship model', *Family Relations*, Vol. 39, pp 81-86.

Hoffman, M. and Hoffman L. (1973), 'The Value of Children to Parents' in Fawcett, J. T. (Ed.), *Psychological Perspectives on Population*, New York: Basic Books.

Hollander, S. (1984), 'Marx and Malthusianism : Marx's secular path of wages' in *American Economic Review*, Vol. 74, No. 1, (Mar) pp139-51.

Houghton, P. and Houghton, D. (1977), *Unfocussed Grief: Responses to Childlessness*, Birmingham Settlement.

Houghton, P. and Houghton, D. (1987), *Coping with Childlessness*, London: Unwin Hyman.

Hull, M. G. R. *et al* (1985), 'Population Study of the causes, treatment and outcome of infertility' *British Medical Journal*, Vol. 14, December.

Humphrey, M. (1969), *The Hostage Seekers: a Study of Childless and Adopting Couples*, London: Longman.

Irvine, D. S. (1994), 'Falling sperm quality', *British Medical Journal*, Vol. 309, pp 476-80.

James, A. and Prout, A. (Eds), (1990), *Constructing and Reconstructing Childhood*, Basingstoke: Falmer Press.

James, P. D. (1994), *Children of Men*, London: Penguin.

Jones, E. (Ed.), (1984), *Social Stigma: The Psychology of Marked Relationships*, New York: W H Freeman,

Kandiyoti, D. (1988), 'Bargaining with Patriarchy', *Gender and Society*, Vol. 2, pp. 274-90.

Keeble, S. (1994), *Infertility, Feminism and the New Technologies*, London: Fabian Society.

Kolenda, P. (1982), 'Pox and the Terror of childlessness', in Preston, J (Ed.), *Mother Worship*, University of North Carolina Press.

Lerner, M. and Miller, D. (1978), 'Just World Research and the Attribution Process', *Psychological Bulletin*, Vol. 85, pp. 1030-1051.

Le Masters, E. E. (1957), 'Parenthood as crisis', *Marriage and Family Living*, Vol. 19, pp. 352-355.

Lorber, J. and Bandlamundi, L. (1993), 'The dynamics of Marital Bargaining in Male Infertility', *Gender and Society*, pp. 32-49, March.

Mahlstedt, P. (1980), 'The psychological component of infertility', *Fertility and Sterility*, Vol, 43, No. 3.

Matthews, R. and Matthews, A. M. (1986), 'Involuntary Childlessness', *Journal of Marriage and the Family*, Vol. 48, pp 641-649, August.

McCracken, G. (1988), *The Long Interview; Qualitative Research Methods*, London: Sage Publications.

McFalls, J. (1979), *Psychopathology and Sub-Fecundity*, New York: Academic Press.

McKee, L. and O'Brien, M. (1982), *The Father Figure*, London: Tavistock.

McNicoll, G. (1975), 'Community Level Population Policy: An Exploration', *Population and Development Review*, Vol. 1, No. 1, pp 1-21.

Miall, C. (1986), 'The stigma of involuntary childlessness', *Social Problems*, Vol. 33, No. 4, April.

Mosher, W. (1982), 'Infertility trends among US couples 1965-76', *Family Planning Perspectives*, Vol. 14.

Person, E. S. (1980), 'Sexuality as the mainstay of identity; psychoanalytic perspectives', *Signs*, Vol. 5.

Philipp, E. (1983), *Childlessness: It's causes and what to do about them*, Hamlyn Paperbacks.

Pfeffer, N. (1994), *The Stork and the Syringe: A Political History of Reproductive Medicine*, Oxford: Polity Press.

Population Investigation Committee Archives, (PIC) PIC V111 1 PIC Papers, London School of Economics.

Russo, N. F. (1976), 'The motherhood mandate', *Journal of Social Issues*, Vol. 32, pp. 143-153, Summer.

Sandelowski, M. (1990), 'Failures of Volition: Female agency and infertility in historical perspective', *Signs*, Vol. 15, pp. 475-90.

Selwyn, J. (1991), 'Applying to adopt , the experience of rejection', *Adoption and Fostering*, Vol. 15, No. 3. pp. 26-29

Selwyn, J. (1994), 'Spies informers and double agents, adoption assessments and role ambiguity', *Adoption and Fostering*, Vol. 18, No. 4, pp. 43-48.

Shaw, C. (1990), 'Fertility assumptions for 1989 based population projections for England and Wales', *Population Trends*, Vol. 61, pp. 17-23.

Smith, J. (1995), 'An offence against nature? Rubbish', *The Guardian*, 22.4.95.

Stafford, M. and Scott, R. (1986), 'Deviance and Social Control', in Ainlay, S. C., Becker, G. and Coleman, L. M., *The Dilemma of Difference*, London: Plenum Press.

Templeton, A., Fraser, C., and Thompson, B. (1990), 'The epidemiology of infertility in Aberdeen', *British Medical Journal*, Vol. 301, pp. 148-152.

Veevers, J. E. (1980), *Childless by Choice,* Toronto: Butterworth.

Veevers, J. E. (1972), 'The violation of fertility mores: voluntary childlessness as deviant behaviour in Boydell' (Ed.), *Deviant Behaviour and Societal Reaction,* New York: Rinehart and Winston.

Warnock, M. (1985), *A Question of Life,* Oxford: Blackwell.

Warner, M. (1993), 'Women against Women in The Old Wives Tales', Petrie, D. (Ed.), *Cinema and the Realms of Enchantment,* British Film Institute, pp. 64 78.

4 I don't eat peas anyway! Classroom stories and the social construction of childhood

Lesley Pugsley, Amanda Coffey and Sara Delamont

Introduction

A considerable amount has been written about the social construction of childhood, but in the main, pedagogical, psychological and sociological accounts have focused on the social world of the child in terms of a deficit model. That is, childhood is seen as an incremental, staged quest toward the ultimate state of Nirvana - adulthood. School days may or may not be the happiest days, but they do represent a large part of childhood, and can be seen as crucial on the way to the goal of adulthood. Yet many of the accounts of school experience are provided from adult perspectives. The stories and narratives of teachers provide us with a very rich account of the school and the classroom (see for example Sikes *et al* 1985, Cortazzi 1992, Goodson 1992). However in these accounts the voices of the children appear almost muted (Ardener 1975) and certainly in the background. There are relatively few studies which have focused on the stories children tell of their own experiences of school. Accordingly, our understanding of the school experience most often originates from adults and their adult concerns.

This chapter takes as its focus the narratives and stories which children and young adults tell and retell of their childhood and their school days. The data are derived from the re-examination of 217 accounts of transfer from primary to secondary school collected from Sixth Form pupils and undergraduates in 1988 and 1989 (Delamont 1989) together with 75 transfer stories collected from undergraduates in 1994 and 1995. The accounts serve to illustrate recurrent themes of childhood concerns and fears about status passage and hierarchy within the school structure, and provide the basis for arguing that children's accounts should be taken seriously.

It has long been acknowledged that schools operate a two tier curriculum, a formal, academic curriculum and an informal one which addresses the traditional socialisation of gender and class. However Best (1983) suggests that there is also a third tier, a well hidden curriculum which the children themselves provide and which serves to allow them to understand how to relate to each other. She argues that children are aware that not only is this curriculum not supplied for them by adults, but it is also one which adults actually seem to avoid. Children therefore are aware that they need to keep it *sub rosa*. One means of access to this hidden curriculum is by *listening* to the stories and legends that children tell each other and *analysing* the content in order to identify any underlying purposes and functions which the stories may have.

Oral subcultures are abundant in schools and they produce a range of stories, many of which are located within the transfer process from primary to secondary school. Versions of these stories are commonplace and widespread throughout the schools in the United Kingdom and doubtless elsewhere too. They are often highly coloured, fantastic and *almost unbelievable,* yet considerable credence is given to these stories by the listeners and the tellers; that is the ten year old and eleven year old children. The world that the narrative describes *is* fantastic, it is dangerous and unknown and the child who enters it, does so as an explorer, and an adventurer and so needs to be prepared to encounter anything, even the *almost* unbelievable. The recognition and analysis of children's stories can provide a real insight into the world of the child and the social construction of adulthood. By encouraging children and young adults to recall the myths, legends and stories which are abundant in school and child culture, adults may share in the world of childhood and create the opportunity to move toward understanding the complex world of children.

The collecting of accounts and stories in the context of social research draws on activity ambiguous in every day life. The story *genre* is a universal social activity. Moreover, all of us, both individually and collectively, use stories to structure life events and activities in the life course. Childhood narrative accounts of the transfer from primary school to secondary school as told by children and retold by young adults, are one such example of a particular kind of narrative, that is the atrocity story or moral fable. The stories told about this transitionary move in the world of childhood underlie the anticipated pitfalls of 'growing up' and of moving to the 'big school'. As such they serve to make a point, provide a moral, or at the very least signpost the way toward a certain construction of young adulthood. We should acknowledge here, of course, that the myths and legends that children tell, and adults retell, of the transfer to secondary

57

schooling are not 'real', or may not be real. That is, they probably do not originate from an actual happening. However we recognise that they may be real in their consequences: of preparing the young child for new roles and new views of the social world they occupy. Narratives can and do create their own reality (Le Borie Burns 1992). The collection of pupils' narrative accounts of 'transfer' stories can therefore inform and develop understanding of how children (and young adults retrospectively) make sense of major events and key points in their childhood.

Transferring to the 'big school'

> ... it had started out as such an adventure, the new bag, the uniform, the bus ride - but the school was so big; I was afraid of getting lost, of not getting to the right lesson, of teachers, of bells ringing, ... I was afraid of everything.

> we were told you would get your head stuck down the toilet every term and the bumps on your birthday. I didn't mind the thought of the bumps, but the toilet one, yuck, No Way!

These are two different accounts taken from pupils' recollections of their feelings, just before and at the start of the period of transfer from primary to secondary school. The first illustrates some of the rational fears which the child might experience on the first day at secondary school and are associated with the natural uncertainties which might commonly accompany any process of moving from the familiar to the strange, from the known to the unknown. Such rational anxieties are common, and most people will be able to identify with the uncertainties which come on the first day at a new job, initial encounters at a club or society, or the entry into a new culture encountered on a foreign holiday. As the raw recruit, the novice, or the outsider, there is a degree of discomfort associated with 'not yet knowing the ropes' and in consequence there is a feeling of difference, of not belonging. Although there are many periods of transition which are acknowledged to be stressful and perhaps daunting, one which is often minimised and 'taken for granted' as just part of growing up, is that of the school transfer from primary to secondary stage. For the pupils concerned, this status passage is viewed with a considerable degree of ambivalence. The prospect is exciting, challenging and stimulating, yet at the same time it represents a source of anxiety, trepidation and in some instances utter dread.

Studies including those by Bryan (1980), Measor and Woods (1986) and the 'Oracle' Project (see for example, Delamont and Galton 1987), have shown that while many pupils readily acknowledge that they have outgrown the primary setting, nevertheless, they still express fears about the move to secondary school. Considerable research attention has focused on the rational fears which children express during the transition period and it is suggested that pupils' anxieties about issues of transfer focus on four general areas of concern, namely; the new school buildings, the curriculum, the teachers and the pupils. Fears concerning the new school building tend to concentrate on their size and the complexities of their layout. Pupils fear that they will get lost as they move around the school, that they will be unable to correctly locate a specific classroom and in consequence will be late for lessons. Fears are also located within curriculum concerns, since they will study a broader range of subjects at secondary level which will be taught in a number of different locations around the school and by a number of different specialist teachers. Pupils will encounter, many for the first time ever, science and language laboratories, information technology stations, domestic science and textile units and art and craft studios. They will be expected to conduct themselves appropriately in each of these strange environments and possibly may need to wear appropriate clothing on such occasions. These considerations provide another source of rational concern which pupils address with a mixture of anticipation and anxiety.

The wider curriculum offered at secondary level also presents the opportunity for the pupils to encounter a greater number of teaching and ancillary staff than at primary level. The subject specialists, the laboratory and computing technicians, heads of departments, teachers with special responsibilities for pastoral care can provide the pupils with cause for concern. Will they remember everyone's name, their subject area and their particular role in the school? Pupils also express fears that they may not 'get on' with all of them. That is they will encounter teachers with whom they will have explicit conflict or disagreement. Bryan (1980), reported that in one case a pupil suggested that having different teachers could be worrying since not all the teachers might be of the same standard and in consequence this could be reflected in the pupils' work. The fourth of the rational fears expressed by the pupils about transfer from primary school to secondary school is concerned with the pupils at the new school. Frequently, secondary school intakes are made up of children from a number of feeder primary schools. For new pupils there are the difficulties of getting to know and establishing friendship groups with children from other primary schools within what might well be a large catchment area. There are also the problems of fitting in with the other children already well established in the secondary school. In consequence, many children express very real fears about being accepted. They fear that they might be singled out, seen as different and possibly bullied or ostracised in consequence.

Plowden (1967) highlighted the importance of continuity and consistency between the different stages of a child's education and since then it has been increasingly acknowledged that there is a vital need to ensure a system of liaison between the primary and secondary schools. There has been a considerable amount of research conducted into effectiveness of pre-transfer initiatives and schools are becoming increasingly more aware of their value in easing the transfer process. Delamont and Galton (1986) looked at six secondary schools in the East Midlands and the strategies which they adopted in order to assist the transition both for the pupils and the parents. Their study identified reciprocal arrangements between feeder primary and the secondary schools for visits, talks and open evenings as some of the various means of easing the period of change. Such initiatives have much to commend them, since they help to overcome many of the fears of the unknown which pupils experience. They address such real concerns as - 'How do I go about getting my lunch? Do I join a queue? Are tables called in turn? Are there special places for different year groups? Where do we do C.D.T. and more to the point, what is it? Do we need special equipment to do House Assembly?' These examples demonstrate the way in which many of the fears which pupils have are located within concerns about the organisation and practice of the new school. They are the rational and accepted concerns which good liaison practice can do much to address and alleviate. However, it can be suggested that there has been little attempt at providing an ethnographic focus on the irrational fears which are installed and supported as a response to the 'urban legends' which are traditionally passed down through generations of school children, just before or during the period of transition.

The second of the two quotations at the beginning of this section, is firmly located within the realms of such urban legends which Brunvand (1984: ix) defines as, 'highly captivating and plausible, but mainly fictional, oral narratives that are widely told as true stories.' He suggests that as part of social group interaction, people enjoy engaging in the recounting and listening to stories. These tales often have a 'scary' theme and while the stories entertain, they may also serve to act as a warning to the listeners of the dangers of the unknown. There is evidence which suggests that the use of such urban legends by older pupils, siblings and neighbourhood children frequently act as a means of alerting younger children to and preparing them for, the dangers which await them on their arrival at the 'big school'.

A rich variety of scary stories are illustrated by Delamont (1989, 1991) and make use of data taken from various studies of pupil transfer, together with stories collected from two hundred and seventeen young adults who reported to her the recollections which they had of their own transition experiences. From these data, Delamont identified five major recurrent themes which exist within the school transfer legends. She classified these into categories:

The Rat myth describes the belief that secondary school science is characterised by the rat dissection (the most lurid of these has the rat alive or pregnant or both!). *The Terrifying Teacher myth* refers to the stories that there will be at least one teacher at the new school who is literally terrifying. *The Five Mile Run myth* denotes the fear of secondary school physical education, of cross country runs in all weathers and with disregard for illness or levels of fitness. *The Violent Gang myth* is concurrent with the move from being senior in the primary school to junior in the secondary school. The belief that violent gangs will be 'out to get you' is usually told and retold by school children. Finally, *The Lavatory/Shower myth* is usually associated with the 'celebration' of birthdays, but can occur in other contexts. Stories of having your head pushed down the lavatory, being forced to take cold showers or being put into a (full) rubbish bin are familiar versions of this.

Delamont (1991) suggests that many of the themes both implicit and explicit in the stories provides evidence regarding the sex roles and sexuality of pupils during early adolescence. The stories are fully chronicled elsewhere, Delamont (1989, 1991) and are not reiterated here. This chapter also goes on to discuss new data, collected from undergraduate students, on the transfer from the primary to secondary school environment.

'I don't eat peas anyway'

In 1994, a group of second year sociology undergraduates were asked to collect transfer stories from either a fellow student, or a pupil currently at secondary school. It must be acknowledged that given their course of study and therefore their prior understanding of the nature of the existing research on school transfer, they did not engage in totally ingenious interviewing and reporting. However, it was interesting to note the consistency with which the earlier identified themes emerged. There were some interesting variations to these stories. The exercise also provided some new and previously unrecorded versions of the urban myths and legends which Delamont and others have classified.

The Rat Myth, emerged as a commonly recurrent theme in the undergraduate accounts and relate to fears which pupils hold regarding the new curriculum which they will encounter in the secondary school. The students reported that pupils were frequently told that they would be required to dissect animals as part of their science lessons, Measor and Woods (1984) noted that boys relished telling these stories about cutting up rats, while girls were scared and squeamish about them. While many of the students recollected having heard they stories, they also noted that in reality, no animal dissection is undertaken unless, or until 'A' level biology is studied. One variation of the Rat Myth which emerged from the students interviews came from 'Ben', a twelve year old, who remembered being told at his primary school that:

> in big school, they get you to dissect fish and some of the boys steal the fish eyes and drop them in with the peas for the school dinners. But that story didn't bother or scare *me*, 'cos I don't eat peas anyway!

The commonly reported legend of the terrifying teacher also appeared in the new stories that were collected. The terrifying teacher myth entails pupils being told that certain members of staff are extremely strict, sometimes it is suggested that this extends almost to the point of *masochism*. There are well chronicled transfer legends which tell tales of pupils being 'beaten up', or 'tied with rope and suspended from the ceiling' if they misbehave in class or infringe minor rules and regulations. The undergraduate accounts revealed several new and different versions of this myth which took the form of stories about:

> Killer Reece, the science teacher, we were warned not to misbehave in his class, or in the corridors or the playgrounds if 'killer' was about. It was never made explicit as to the fate of any pupils who did behave badly, but the name was enough to put you off!

One undergraduate, Jeff, recalled the story told about; 'Mr Croate, who would string pupils up on butchers hooks in his cupboard and then eat them!'. Jeff noted that he remembers that while he '*absolutely did not* believe' this story, he was nevertheless scared of Mr Croate for a long while and then never really 'took' to him. Possibly this myth served to feed into a general apprehension about the new teachers to be encountered at secondary school. One undergraduate recalled being told by older pupils at her secondary school to, 'watch out for Peahead and Bunhead', and noted that 'I don't remember Peaheads' real name, but Bunhead was.. uh..oh yes, Mrs Roberts, they warned me to 'watch out for *her*...she keeps telling you what to do.'

Measor and Woods (1984), found that the myth about cross country running is used to reflect both the ways in which secondary school places heavier physical demands upon its students and sanctions them. It also serves to indicate that there is a masculinity associated with the school culture, which demands a need to save face within the peer group. One version of this myth was reported by Ben, who recalled being told that:

> no matter what the weather, even if it snowed, we would have to run to the park, run around it and run back without stopping. They said that if you stopped you just got left behind!

Delamont (1989) found that myths or legends about 'the rat', 'the teacher' and the 'run' were recounted by both boys and girls. All three shared common theories about the nature of the curriculum and the teaching staff in the secondary school. In contrast the 'violent gang' and 'lavatory' myths are associated with the anticipation of pupil culture at the secondary school. The Violent gang stories serve to 'warn' new pupils about the older, often violent pupils and the activities they engage which are specifically aimed at hurting or humiliating the new students. Ben remembered that:

> we were told that Form 3 boys would hang you by your trouser belt loops from the coat pegs in the cloakrooms and leave you so you would miss lessons. Or else they'd beat you up and shove you in one of the tin lockers in there.

Jeff remembered being told that when you went to High School:

> you didn't trust the older pupils, they were out to get you, so you couldn't ask them for help if you got lost 'cause they would probably send you the wrong way on purpose.

One particularly unpleasant version of the 'Violent Gang' myth was reported by a 14 year old boy, interviewed by one undergraduate. He recalled that in junior school he was told that when you were in the secondary school:

> some guys would come and slit your mouth and then grab your testicles and try to castrate you, you wouldn't get castrated, but you would be so scared you would scream and split your mouth up to your ears ... it really scared me and I believed it for ages after I got there.

Delamont (1989) has argued that these gang myths offer exaggerated versions of bullying activities which are widely believed to occur to newcomers to a school. They are frequently located in cloakrooms and toilet areas, where there are limited amounts of teacher supervision.

The final common theme is that of the Lavatory Myth and this Delamont (1989) argues has been around for a very long time. It is associated not only with bullying but also with fears of contamination and the defilement of particular events and special occasions. Many of the stories connected with the Lavatory Myth refer to pupils being subjected to a 'bog wash' on their birthdays for example. During their time at primary school, a birthday is marked out as a happy occasion, the class sing to the child, perhaps a small gift presented by the teacher and the pupil is made to feel 'special' on this day. Delamont (1989) indicated that the myth is used to illustrate the possibilities that at secondary school, pollution and humiliation may well be associated with a celebratory event. Measor and Woods (1984) associate this particular myth with the inversion of status which is an integral part of any such transfer. Ben was told that 'on your birthday bigger boys will grab your head and flush it down the loo, even if there is *something* still down there!'. While a fourteen year old admitted he had heard tales in his primary school that 'you would get your head stuck down the toilet every term and the bumps on your birthday' he commented that 'while he didn't mind the bumps, the toilet thing... yuck. No Way.' A different version of the Lavatory Myth came from a female undergraduate student who had attended a comprehensive school in a coastal town in South Wales. Here pupils were told that they would be 'egged' on their birthdays and on the last day of the school year. This 'egging' involved having raw eggs and flour thrown at the individual by a gang of pupils in an attempt to both humiliate and soil that student. There was also another myth at this particular school associated with 'snogging'. New pupils were told by older pupils that certain areas of the playgrounds were 'out of bounds' to them, since this was where the older pupils went with their boyfriends and girlfriends. The penalty which would be imposed on any junior pupils found to be snooping in this area was that they would be forced to kiss someone they didn't like. The respondent noted that it was this particular myth which caused her the greatest degree of concern, because she heard it from her cousin, someone she 'believed beyond any doubt'.

Conclusions

Anxieties are an integral part of any status passage and it can be suggested that an analysis of the *rites de passage* of pupil transfer can be presented within the theoretical framework of structural anthropology (Delamont 1991). School transfer involves the pupil in a move from the top of one hierarchy within the primary school, to the bottom of another at secondary school. The structuralist approach adopted by Levi-Strauss (1966, 1967), Leach (1969) and Douglas (1975a, 1975b) provides a useful analytical approach. Structuralists draw distinctions between 'outsiders' and 'insiders', and 'the knowing' and 'the unknowing'. Within each of the myths and legends of transfer there is a persistent theme of binary discrimination. Every story carries with it a message about the normative values of society and serves to offer an indication of the rules and norms which apply to each new situation. The myths serve to warn the novice, by suggesting that on transfer, the younger, weaker members enter a situation which is potentially dangerous. Such a warning, together with the possible means of avoidance, are relayed to the newcomer, the 'outsider' by an 'insider'. Leach (1969) argues that a three part structure exists which allows the bearer of the warning to act as mediator between the newcomer and the aggressor by providing within the warning advice on the means of escape. Implicit within this warning is the message that not all 'insiders' are potential aggressors, since some 'insiders' may already be known to the newcomer, either as relatives or friends.

Pupils who are about to transfer from a primary to a secondary school are inevitably faced with a major status reversal; the eleven year old must acknowledge and come to terms with this prospect of change. The familiar, mainly female dominated (most teaching and auxiliary staff at primary schools are women), small, secure local school will be replaced with attendance at a large, unfamiliar, male dominated school, often located a considerable distance from the child's home. The 'big fish' from the local pool must struggle to come to terms with being a very small and insignificant fish in a cosmopolitan lagoon. The perpetuation of the urban legends associated with the transition period of school transfer serves to prepare pupils for a major status passage. They help to acquaint children with the rules and regulations inherent in a larger organisation and serve as a useful and powerful method of social control.

Myths and stories are and remain a vivid part of the culture of childhood and of young adulthood. What we have suggested here is that such stories and myths should be listened to and be taken seriously by adults. While the stories themselves may be mythical or irrational, the fears that accompany such stories may be very rational to a young child. By listening to childrens' stories more closely and analysing what we, as adults, may see as 'irrational' fears, the fate of pupils like Ben might be avoided. Ben never admitted at the time that he was concerned about the stories he had heard in connection with secondary school because he 'knew that the teacher would say they weren't true, just to stop us being scared, but they wouldn't have really *explained* them'.

Analysis of childrens' narratives can be used to explore how childhood is constructed and how it is understood by children themselves. This can open up the exploration of power within the classroom and the related issue of gender. Transfer stories in particular might also have policy implications. The move to secondary school is a key stage in a young persons life. A better understanding of how it is constructed and anticipated by children themselves may make the move a more positive one.

References

Ardener, S. (1975), *Perceiving Women* London: Malaby.

Best, R. (1983), *We've All Got Scars* Indiana: Indiana University Press.

Brunvand, J. (1984), *The Choking Doberman*. New York: Norton.

Bryan, K.A. (1980), Pupil Perceptions of Transfer. in A. Hargreaves & L. Tickle (eds.) *Middle Schools*. London: Harper Row.

Cortazzi, M. (1992), *Narrative Analysis*. London: Falmer.

Delamont, S. (1989), '*The Nun in The Toilet: urban legends and educational research*.' in Qualitative Studies in Education. 1989 Vol. 2. No.3.

Delamont, S. (1991), *The Hit List and Other Horror Stories, Sex Roles and School Transfer*. Sociological Review. 42.

Delamont, S. & Galton, M. (1986), *Inside The Secondary Classroom*. London: Routledge and Kegan Paul.

Goodson, I. (1992), *Studying Teachers' Lives.* London: Routledge.

Le Borie Burns, T. (1992), *On Becoming The Devil in The Dance Hall* in FOAFTALE NEWS. No.25 March 1992.

Measor, L. & Woods, P. (1984), *Changing Schools.* Milton Keynes: Open
University Press.
Sikes, P. Measor, L. & Woods, P. (1985), *Teacher Careers.* London:
Falmer.

5 Growing up respectable

Odette Parry

This chapter is based upon data collected as part of research which examined how naturists (nudists) constructed and sustained a version of their activities which contradicted the 'common sense wisdom' that public nudity is unrespectable. This account explores both the experiences of children who accompany their parents to naturist clubs and their wider role in the construction and maintenance of naturism as a 'respectable' pursuit.

The theoretical perspective with which this research is most closely allied is symbolic interactionism because it rejects a view of the social world as stable and unchanging in favour of a world which takes it's meaning from the interpretation and interactional flow of social action. The methodological approach was informed by the principles of naturalism and the main research method was participant observation (1). For reasons which will be become more apparent as this account unfolds, participant observation in naturist clubs encountered some unusual research problems. The main problem was a cultural one in that eye contact between members was taboo (it was not a context where individuals were encouraged to watch each other) and this rendered observation as the sole research method untenable. For this reason, and the obvious advantages to be gained by triangulation, observation was complemented by interviews, on the club premises, with adult members of the club. The interviews were semi-structured and included both closed and open ended responses. However their main advantage was that the use of schedules legitimated the research in the eyes of members and allowed me a measure of freedom, to approach people, which I would not have otherwise enjoyed. In the clubs which I visited it was agreed with club secretaries and official naturist representatives that, although I had the run of the club, I could only talk to *adults* who consented to be interviewed.

Naturist clubs in Britain are affiliated to a national organisation The Central Council of British Naturism (C.C.B.N.), which itself is affiliated to an international body, the International Naturist Federation. It was through the C.C.B.N. that I gained access to official naturist records and ultimately to the club which accepted me as a member. In recognition of the principle of informed consent, and with the approval of the C.C.B.N., I observed and interviewed in the club where my membership was accepted and also, through a reciprocal agreement, in other clubs in England and Wales who were willing to allow a researcher on to their premises. I felt this was particularly important given that one of the most forceful criticisms of ethnographic research is it's questionable generalisability.

Whilst the majority of my fieldwork was conducted at the club which I joined, visiting other clubs allowed me to theoretically sample other sites and test out working hypotheses as they were developed and grounded in the data collection process. The only conditions of membership were that I protected my anonymity of clubs and members who I met in them and that, like everyone else at the clubs which I visited, I took my clothes off.

In Western civilised society public nudity is culturally taboo and greeted with social disapprobation. That is not to say nakedness is always unacceptable, but it's acceptability is dependent upon the contexts in which it occurs. Acceptable nudity is confined to the private rather than the public setting; for example the bedroom, changing room, and bathroom. Where the rules which define when and where nudity is acceptable and disregarded then nudity becomes 'matter out of place' (Douglas 1966 & 1978) and by default unclean, dirty and indecent.

Attitudes towards nudity are at least partly informed by a perceived relationship between nakedness and sexuality (Polheimus 1974) and hence sex has been routinely posited (by non-naturists) as the motivating factor behind forms of social nudity':

> It is precisely because the nude body is extremely sexually
> exciting to people in a society which has been covered up for
> millennia that people want to uncover in the first place.
>
> (Douglas, 1977:225)

Taboos about nudity make the practice of naturism a potential focus of public disapproval or moral outrage. Because, however most naturism takes place outside of the public gaze (behind high walls and locked gates) non-naturists have little contact or exposure to naturists beliefs or practices. Where exposure occurs then public condemnation follows. A measure of this condemnation can be gauged from the national reaction to an attempt (organised by the C.C.B.N.) in the late seventies to claim several stretches of British coast line as nude bathing areas. While having limited success the campaign focused public attention upon naturist activities and unleashed a moral outrage against the perpetrators.

The highly publicised arguments for and against nude beaches came to a head in the English seaside resort of Hayling Island. Those in favour of opening a nude beach included several local councillors, the Secretary for Trade for Hayling Island and some local naturists. Not all naturist club members in the Hayling area were in favour of official nude beaches; some were wary of exposing their activities to an unsympathetic public.

The voice of the opposition was most forcibly heard through the local newspaper *'The Hayling Islander'* and particularly in a column written by a former town councillor. The newspaper claimed support of a thousand local residents in opposition to the nude beach and a member of the local clergy.

> Judging by our heavy post bag on the subject of nude bathing, one this is certain. Hayling people don't want bare bodies.
>
> (Hayling Islander, 1979)

View points expressed by readers which included descriptions of the campaign as, 'Just one more attempt by communists and Marxists to destroy all that is decent', and clothing as, 'the last physical barrier between civilised man and animals', particularly highlighted children as a vulnerable group:

> We all need to shake off this apathy which is threatening to drown us and our children in a sea of permissiveness,

and described the imminent danger of children witnessing 'couples copulating in public'.

In retaliation, the C.C.B.N. asserted that far from being a corrupting influence, naturism is both natural and beneficial for families in general and children in particular,

> We believe there is a significant mental and moral benefit to those - especially children - who participate in naturist recreation. We have established over an ample length of experience that children of naturist parents do not become delinquent, that the divorce rate among naturists is far below the national average and that naturists generally are, in simple words, happier people.
>
> (C.C.B.N., 1979)

Research (Edgerton 1979) has demonstrated how potentially 'dangerous' social situations can be constructed or re-interpreted in ways which render them 'safe' for participants. For example there have been previous studies of naturists, carried out in North America and Canada (Weinburg, 1967, 1968, 1970; Screaton-Page, 1971), which relied primarily upon self administered questionnaires with little or no observation in clubs. They did however agree that naturists constructed a 'situated morality' in their clubs. This 'situation morality' rejected the view that naturism was indecent and anaesthetising the nude/sexual 'appresentation' (Schutz 1962). This was mainly achieved through the recruitment policies of clubs.

Data from my observation and interviewing in British clubs supports these findings in that naturists constructed a version of 'decent exposure' through the guide lines of the C.C.B.N., the recruitment policies of member clubs and the practices of members themselves. As we shall see, naturist children play a pivotal role in the construction and maintenance of this decent exposure.

Naturists described the boundaries which informed 'decent exposure' and also the individuals who could legitimately participate. Hence the C.C.B.N. maintained that naturism was a 'naked but non-sexual' activity which occurred outside, in amenable weather conditions, in daylight hours or designated premises. They also prescribed naturism as 'an activity to be enjoyed by all family members' and operated a recruitment policy which discriminated against some applicants in favour of others.

The recruitment policies of C.C.B.N. affiliated clubs favoured applications from families with children and discriminated against applications from single men. The C.C.B.N.'s definition of naturism as a 'naked but non-sexual activity to be enjoyed by the whole family', held the key to this recruitment policy. Married men were not allowed to join C.C.B.N. clubs unless their spouses agreed to join also. When a married couple joined a club then both partners were expected to visit the club together, and they were encouraged to bring their children, where applicable. Of the ten thousand C.C.B.N. membership (either families or individuals), at the time of my research, the Council estimated that 75% were families who visited clubs accompanied by children, 15% were childless couples, 8.7% were single men and 1.3% were single women (2).

The stratification of club applicants favoured families with children then (in descending order) childless couples, single women and single men (3). However although families were seen as the most desirable members and single men were seen as the least desirable, clubs received many thousands of applications to join from single men every year.

> We always get far more applications from single men that
> we do from single women. If fact we rarely get applications
> from single women which is a shame. Although we do
> accept a number of single men we like to balance it with
> single women, because an overwhelming number of single
> men may appear threatening to the married men members
> and their families.
>
> (C.C.B.N. Committee Member)

Data from the interviews suggested that members could be categorised according to their reasons for joining the club. The first of the three categories which I identified comprised those individuals who wanted to join and did so under no compulsion. The second category comprised those individuals who were persuaded, cajoled or bullied to join by a significant other. The third category comprised those who really had no choice in the matter. The first category, was made up almost entirely of men (with the exception of two women who had been members as children and who elected to join again as adults). The second category was entirely made up of the wives of men belonging to the first category and the final group were children, enrolled by their parents, with no say in the matter.

Those members who were least interested in joining the club initially experienced the most problems of adjustment upon joining. Compared to the men who I interviewed, and contrary to the C.C.B.N. (1978) claims:

> It's like jumping into a swimming pool. Shocking for the
> first 30 seconds, comfortable and soothing from them on.

women described the period of adjustment to naturism as both difficult and protracted. Many talked about their awareness of social disapprobation and their reticence to take on board a naturist perspective of nudism. Many also remembered clearly, and recalled, their first club visit and particularly their distaste in publicly removing their clothes:

> I really didn't want to join but my husband was so interested
> in it and he just went on and on at me until I said OK When
> I first came to the club I felt so self conscious and
> embarrassed and I hated taking off my clothes. I didn't
> know where to look.

I found I was able to identify with the anxiety which women described. My only reason for being at the club was to collect data. A condition of my membership was that I should adhere to rules of the club which insisted upon nudity. Initially I experienced difficulty in coming to terms with this participation and it was not until well into the season that I overcame my unease in undressing among strangers (Parry, 1987).

Nevertheless the interview data suggested that after the initial adjusting period women were among the club's most ardent supporters (4).

> Well I hated it at first. Taking off your clothes in front of strangers was just something you didn't do. Well I didn't anyway. But now I think it's OK There's nothing indecent about it. We spend a lot of time at the club and I like the fact that I feel the children are very safe here and we're doing something as a family.

Assisting this adjustment were a number of benefits of membership which appeared to serve women over men. The first of these described by female respondents was that they perceived the club as a safe environment for their children.

> I don't have to worry about the kids here. I know they are perfectly safe. If we were at home they'd want to be out playing on the street or over the park and you can't keep an eye on them all the time. Here I feel everyone watches out for them. It's a bit like a big family.

Women felt children were safe because applicants for club membership were rigorously vetted. The procedure for club membership was both protracted and thorough. Applicants were required to apply to the C.C.B.N. who forwarded their application to a club in the vicinity of the applicant. The club secretary and committee assessed the application and, if agreed on his/her suitability, contacted the applicant by letter. The applicant was then required to sign a declaration that he/she had no other reason for joining a club other than the pursuit of naturism and that if accepted as a member would never reveal the location of the club to non-members. If still satisfied the committee sent a representative to the applicant's home. This was felt particularly important in the case of married couples or family applications because the committee would need to establish whether the applicant's spouse (and children) would be prepared to visit the club of a regular basis. Where the applicant was single the club secretary arranged to meet him/her *en route* to the club (although the actual location of the club would not be revealed at this stage). The club secretary then drove to the appointed meeting place and chose whether or not to identify him/her self to the applicant. The applicant would then be interviewed and if suitable would be invited to follow the secretary to the club. This procedure was the one adopted in the case of my own application to join a club.

The application procedure and applicant vetting was more rigorous for single male applicants who were required to join the C.C.B.N. and an associate (non-club) member for several seasons prior to visiting a club.

Another reason why women claimed to value membership was that clubs were relatively inexpensive to join. Family units (of whatever size) paid the same subscription as childless couples and singles. The cost per head for large families was therefore low. A third reason, relating to this, was that clubs were very pleasant environments. Many had been established for decades and owned their own land, or alternatively paid a peppercorn rent for well appointed and extensive grounds. They also boasted good facilities; swimming pools, games courts, caravan parking in some cases and club houses. In many ways membership could be likened to that of a superior leisure club and at a fraction of the cost.

Many of the women interviewed also claimed that joining the club had increased the amount of 'quality' time which the family spent together.

> We spend a lot more time together as a family since we joined the club. My husband doesn't go off to golf so much and the kids aren't off playing with their friends.

Unlike the married women I interviewed, the husbands appeared to have little or no problem in adjusting to the club. Most said it had been their idea to join the club with a few describing it as a joint decision (although none of the women had described it as a joint decision). When asked whey they wanted to become naturists the majority of men claimed that it made them 'feel free', as if the release from clothing liberated them from those restrictions they felt characterised their non-naturist identities. In fact this is the position adopted by the C.C.B.N., who claim,

> when we take off our clothes we also take off any phoney postures and status symbols of the everyday world.
>
> (C.C.B.N., 1979)

In contrast the club benefits which women described were very pragmatic and included safety for children, the cost, the facilities and family relationships. The men cited less pragmatic reasons and related more to the symbolic gestures like 'freedom', and 'release'. This is interesting in that whilst the club provided freedom from clothing there were numerous club rules and regulations, both stated and implicit, which prescribed appropriate behaviour in the club. Whereas stated regulations included the 'nudity rule' (prescribing where clothing was inappropriate) and the 'anonymity rule' (proscribing members from giving the location of the club to non-members) others which were not stated governed behaviour inside the club. For example adult members of the club were never seen running (except while engaged in court games), jumping, dancing or exhibiting any other 'uncontrolled' movement at any time. This type of behaviour among adults was not seen as appropriate inside the club. Interaction between any member and a spouse (of the opposite sex) of another member (except where all spouses were present) was taboo. Equally it was not acceptable for members to interact with the children of other members unless the children were supervised by their parents. As already intimated, staring at other members was interpreted as voyeuristic and hence not acceptable behaviour.

Whilst overt sexual behaviour was not explicitly dealt with in the rules of the club, in their club information leaflet (Dare to Go Bare), the C.C.B.N. noted that where 'physical reaction' did occur then it could be swiftly remedied by a 'quick dip' in the swimming pool. Only one of the forty men I interviewed said that he joined the club because he thought it would be sexy (5).

The men tended not to site benefits for children but that may reflect the tendency for child rearing and children's affairs to be seen as 'women's work' (Oakley, 1974). What was more interesting about their responses was that they clearly contradicted the reality of club experience. While citing 'freedom' and 'release', rules and regulations governing behaviour inside the club were arguably more stringent and restrictive than those characterising interaction outside the club.

Naturist children were exempt from many of the implicit rules which restricted adult behaviour in the club. Although they were expected to conform to the nudity rule, they were free to run around the club and play with other children freely on the sun lawn.

Members themselves sustained 'decent exposure', in their everyday behaviour inside the club and, by erecting strong boundaries around their activities. The boundaries which members erected informed their patterns of disclosure (Davis, 1971) and these patterns were an extension of the physical boundaries (high walls and locked gates) which protected the activities of members from the non-naturist gaze. Inside the club, members addressed each other by first name only and were expected to refrain from sharing information about their non-naturist identities with other members

(6). Similarly outside the club members were wary about disclosing their naturist activities to non-naturists. Many of the naturists who were interviewed owned to being highly secretive about their activities to non-club members to the extent that several couples told me that their teenage children had not been told. These couples had become naturist converts when their children were late adolescents and rationalised their secrecy:

> There didn't seem to be any reason to tell them. They wouldn't want to come to the club. They do their own thing anyway. I think they would think it was a bit weird.

I was given similar accounts by members who had not disclosed their activities to parents, colleagues, friends or neighbours. Sometimes lack of disclosure involved complicated and deceitful strategies to avoid discovery:

> We told the neighbours we'd joined a caravan club. Well it is near enough to the truth isn't it. I felt rotten though especially as they kept dropping hints about how they might like to join as well. It's difficult really because they're friends as well as neighbours...

The disclosure patterns of members indicated their awareness of social disapprobation.

> they think we're bearded cranks behind walls.
>
> (C.C.B.N. Regional Secretary)

However, not all members of the club were equally aware of these taboos. Many of the children at the club remained unaware of the strategies which supported and protected naturism from the antipathy of outsiders.

In the club which I belonged to the majority of younger couples who visited the club regularly throughout the summer were accompanied by children. There were always children present at the club when I visited, their ages ranging from young babies to approximately thirteen years. There was a noticeable absence of children from the early teenage years upward.

Parents and club officials who I interviewed explained how whereas at a young age children enjoyed visiting the club, at the onset of puberty most children ceased to visit. The prevailing view among parents was that children, towards the onset of puberty and after, were sensitive to changes

76

in the physical body and became shy and unhappy at the prospect of taking their clothes off at the club.

Some respondents, whose children had left the club, described their children as sensitive and wary of appearing different from their peers; other children who did not belong to naturist families. A woman whose son had stopped visiting the club explained,

> He was perfectly happy coming with us because he had many friends at the club. But then he decided he didn't want to come any more. I think it started in the showers at school when other boys noticed he didn't have the white strip that they had. He got teased about it and when he told them about the club they weren't very nice about it. They called him names and all that. He got upset and he just stopped coming. Just like that. We couldn't persuade him to stay. He never mentions the club now although he knows we still visit.

The club appeared to provide a protective shell for children, in which adults presented naturism as a natural and normal activity. This protective time capsule meant children were not exposed to alternative non-naturist versions of nudity, or the force of social disapprobation.

However once the attention of others was alerted to their activities and they were challenged with an alternative view point of naturism, the protective shell of the club was shattered. This can be likened to what Goffman (1968) has described as a moral experience. Those children who accompanied their naturist parents became socialised into the club and at the same time learned the standards of non-naturist society against which they fell short (Goffman 1963). The moral dilemma occurred where the two conflicting accounts of social nudism met. At this juncture children decided which version of naturism they would accept and which they would reject.

The discovery that naturism was not acceptable outside the club was followed by a period during which children attempted to conform to the demands of both versions. Whereas the younger children at first appeared oblivious to their nudity and the nakedness of other children, the older children employed strategies aimed at concealing their activities from their non-naturist peers. I frequently observed the older children lying naked on the sun lawn using towels to cover parts of their bodies. When I asked an adult member why older children in the club did this she said:

> They don't want to seem different from their friends at
> school. If they have the 'white bits' the other kids have then
> they won't be accused or made fun of for being different.
> Children hate to be seen as different. They will go to great
> lengths to be seen the same as the other children, because
> children can be very cruel.

This strategy was only partly effective in that children inevitably moved around the club and swam in the pool without their protective cover (7). The club secretary explained that 'covering' was a temporary measure which many of the older children adopted before eventually they stopped visiting the club at all. In most cases, he explained, pressure from outside the club, and particularly peers, prevailed and children stop visiting the club.

Although I did not interview children at the club (for reasons given earlier) I did interview three adult naturists who had been members as children. In all three cases these members had left the club at puberty and had not rejoined until well into their twenties. All three talked about the difficulties of remaining in the club once they had been 'discovered' by their non naturist peers. Apart from the eagerness to disassociate themselves from an activity which was censured by peers they also described how, at puberty, they were developing other interests which were located outside of the club and resented the time which they were expected to spend at the club with their parents.

> There would be arguments because my parents wanted me to
> go to the club but I wanted to go to the beach with my
> friends. There were a group of us from school who used to
> hang out at the beach on weekends. I felt at a disadvantage
> in this group because of the periods of time I had to spend at
> the club.

The decision to leave the club appeared therefore to be motivated by several considerations. The two most important considerations described by parents, club officials and ex-child naturists were awareness of social disapprobation and peer pressure. Both of these reasons related to children's relationships outside the club. It may be that relationships inside the club, coupled with sensitivity to physical bodily changes, were equally or more important to children's discomfort in the club. In a setting which divorces sexuality from nudity it is perhaps unlikely that members would allow any aspect of sexuality to inform their accounts of club related behaviour to any extent.

However observation data did suggest that older children, whilst at the club, were not uncomfortable in their relationships with other children or adults. Even where children covered parts of the body when laying on the sun lawn, those precautions were discarded when they ran around the club in play with other children. The data suggests therefore that leaving the club is partly a function of the inability of older children to sustain behaviour which will disguise their naturist activities from non-naturist peers.

In summary, the data showed how naturists engaged in the social construction of respectability. They did this by creating a 'situation morality' which rejected the 'taken for granted' relationship between nudity and sex. This 'situated morality' was reinforced through the policies of the C.C.B.N., the recruitment policies of clubs and the activities of their members.

Fundamental to their version of 'decent exposure' was the central role played by naturist children. Naturism was defined, by the C.C.B.N. and it's member clubs, as an activity 'to be enjoyed by all the family' and children were singled out as the primary beneficiaries of it's mental and moral advantages.

Discussion

Research on naturists and their children has implications for the study of adolescents and child-rearing practices. It has been argued by Wyness (1994) that the literature in this area tends to focus upon the parents and in particular upon their anxieties about their sense of their self worth as parents (Harris 1983; Seabrook 1982). This is both at the expense of understanding parental anxiety about how their children will negotiate the social world outside of the family and of studies which attempt to locate children in the context of these experiences.

Naturist parents, especially mothers, valued the club because they felt it provided a protected and safe environment for their children. They stressed the advantages of a recruitment policy which vetted applicants and protected the balance of membership in favour of families and discriminated against single males. Furthermore the situated morality of the club protected members and their children from the antagonistic gaze of non-naturism.

The data indicated that whereas naturist mothers rated their children's safety highly among the advantages of membership, men had quite different reasons than their wives for joining clubs. The data strongly suggested to me that the men had expectations of naturism (which were loosely related to freedom from cultural and sexual mores) before joining which were not in fact borne out in actual experience. The advantages for women however offset the disappointment of their spouses and (particularly as both spouses must attend the club together) in many cases family membership endured as a function of the positive experiences of these women.

Naturist parents did not appear to be dependent upon their children as a means for assessing their moral self worthiness. When their children rejected naturism and refused to visit the club, parents did not interpret this as in any way threatening to their own self esteem. Indeed many remained as members of the club after their children had left, and some remained long enough to see their children rejoin as adults.

An interesting point to emerge from Wyness's own study of parenting was the pragmatic way in which parents appeared to define the process of moral development. Whereas social theories on child development have tended to view character formation taking place within an idealised and stable society (Riesman 1990; Lash 1977; Bergers 1983), Wyness's study suggests that parents interpret the outside world as fraught with physical and moral dangers. Parental anxiety can therefore be interpreted as a function of their concern about their children's abilities to negotiate a clear path through the real hazards which they will face in society.

Naturist adults maintained their own moral worthiness through the construction of 'decent exposure'. They justified the inclusion of children by reference both to this moral phenomenon and to their own anxieties about the physical (non-naturist) world. Observations of the children suggested however that they were orchestrators of their own moral destinies who actively assessed the moral and physical advantages and disadvantages of naturism as they negotiated a clear path through the hazards of growing up.

This account has been primarily based upon participant observation and while it has included some interviewing, the data on children has been largely derived from either parents' descriptions or observation. That children have remained silent (if visible) has raised some problems for the analysis. The first of these is the danger of accepting that children shared the perceptions that were ascribed to them by their parents. This is particularly poignant given that children emerged as crucial to naturists' definition of 'decent exposure'.

It is in any case precarious to ascribe meanings to the actions of individuals where these cannot be back up with verbal descriptions from the respondents themselves. These problems highlighted the necessity to triangulate the research in ways available to the researcher. Hence the data for this research was derived from numerous sources including, interviews with adult club members, club officials, and C.C.B.N. committee members. Observation data in clubs was collected and the official C.C.B.N. records were examined.

A particular weakness of the research was that data provided from all these sources shared a similar, if not identical, perspective on naturism as a respectable activity. There were few available sources which counterbalanced this perspective. At the time of the research one alternative perspective on nudity was provided through public reaction to the British Nude Beach Campaign and this data was utilised accordingly.

Weaknesses aside, the methods used in the research afforded far greater insight into the construction of club morality than previous accounts of naturism based solely upon postal questionnaires. Membership itself was a 'union ticket' to acceptance. In the eyes of the respondents, by taking my clothes off I became a naturist first and foremost and a researcher second. Undoubtedly my acceptance by other members afforded me access to much richer data than would otherwise been available.

However becoming an insider caused some difficulties of both a personal and professional nature. Whilst coping with the moral dilemmas which I felt were a function of my participation in naturist activities I was simultaneously under pressure from instrumental deadlines to complete postgraduate research. We have noted that women members took the longest to adjust to club naturism, and in this respect I was no exception. My boyfriend disapproved, my parents remained in blissful ignorance, some of my colleagues were titillated by the choice of topic (and method) and my supervisor at times expressed concern over my welfare.

Notes

(1)   Most of the fieldwork for the study was carried out in the summer of 1980. I became a member of a naturist club in May 1980 and carried out particular observation throughout May, June, July and August of that year. Most of the observation took place at the club which I actually joined but during the course of the summer I also visited several other clubs in which I carried out observation.

During the summer I also interviewed seventy naturists on club premises.

(2)   These figures were quoted by a C.C.B.N. official and were based upon data from the clubs collected in 1971 and published by the North Kent Club.

(3)   Earlier research on North American and Canadian naturists (Weinburg 1967, 1968 & 1970 and Screaton Page 1971) reflected a slightly different pattern of membership stratification which favours childless families over families with children and yet which still accords least status to single males. This reflects the fact that ownership of North American and Canadian clubs is largely commercial whereas in Britain, clubs tend to be co-operatively owed by members. Whereas commercial clubs (while maintaining a preference for couples over singles, and particularly over single males) prefer childless couples who pay the same subscriptions as families but who are less drain upon resources. Despite international differences in member status, it is single males have the least status of all membership groups.

(4)   I was not allowed access to membership lists and therefore interviews were restricted to current members who visited clubs. I was unable therefore to interview women who did not adjust to the club and who left as a consequence. However I was assured by C.C.B.N. officials, club secretaries and members of clubs that the attrition rate of members was low, membership turnover was slow and membership waiting lists were long. The relative ease with which I joined was due to the fact that I was a single female applicant. Single females, as I point out in the chapter, are popular with club committees because they are felt to balance single male membership, and hence provide a measure of membership equilibrium.

(5)   This respondent was unusual in that whilst married, he usually visited the club without his wife, but accompanied by his children. His presence at the club did actually cause some problems for me in that the committee members knew he was a lecturer in the same faculty of the university which I attended. Although I was unaware that he was a naturist and a member of the club, until just prior to joining, I was warned, by the club secretary, against appearing familiar in any way with him.

(6)   When joining the club I was instructed that I should provide my own transport to and from the premises and I was actively discouraged (warned off) from accepting lifts from other members.

(7)   All clubs have rules about nudity. In some clubs (due to comfort) partial dress is allowed. In others (like the club I joined) when it becomes uncomfortably cold members are expected to get dressed and leave. However where partial dress is accepted, the 'non-naturist' norms governing partial dress are reversed. That is both men and women (except when menstruating) are expected to cover themselves above the waist only.

References

Bergers, D. & P. (1983), *The War Over the Family: Capturing Middle Ground*, Harmondsworth, Penguin.

Central Council of British Naturism, (1978), *Bare With Us*, Orpington, C.C.B.N. Publications.

Central Council of British Naturism, (1978), *Dare To Go Bare*, Orpington, C.C.B.N. Publications.

Central Council of British Naturism, (1979), *British Naturism Handbook*, Orpington, C.C.B.N. Publications.

Douglas, J. E. (1977), *The Nude Beach*, Newbury, Sage.

Douglas, M. (1966), *Purity and Danger*, London, Routledge and Kegan Paul.

Douglas, M. (1978), *Rules and Meanings*, Harmondsworth, Penguin.

Davis, P. (1981), *Hide and Clique: Structural Aspects of Disclosure of a Discreditable Identity*, (Paper given at a University of Wales Symposium, Gregynog).

Edgerton, R. B. (1979), *Alone Together*, USA: University of California Press.

Goffman, E. (1976), *Stigma: Notes on the Management of a Spoiled dentity*, Harmondsworth, Penguin.

Harris, C.C. (1983), 'The Changing Relation between Family and Societal Form in Western Society', in M. Anderson (ed) *Sociology of the Family*, Harmondsworth, Penguin.

Hayling Islander (1979), Editorial on Nudism, *Hayling Islander*, February.

Ilford, F. et al (1964), *Social Nudism in America*, New Haven College and University Press.

Lash, C. (1977), *Haven in a Heartless World: The Family Besieged*, New York, Basic Books.

Lofland, J. (1971), *Analysing Social Settings*, Belmont, Wadsworth.

North Kent Sun Club (1971), *Family Naturism*, Orpington, C.C.B.N.

Oakley, A. (1974), *The Sociology of Housework*, London, Martin Robertson.

Parry, O. (1982), *Campaign For Respectability: A Study of Organised British Naturism*, Unpublished MPhil Thesis, University of Wales, Cardiff.

Parry, O. (1987), Uncovering the Ethnographer. In McKeganey, N. and Cunningham-Burley, S. (eds), *Enter The Sociologist*, Aldershot, Avebury.

Polheimus, T. (1974), *Body Systems: Towards an Anthropology of the Human Body*, Unpublished MPhil Thesis, University of London.

Reisman, D. (1950), *The Lonely Crowd*, Yale University Press, New Haven.

Seabrook, J. (1982), *Working Class Childhood*, London, Gollancz.

Schutz, A. (1962), *Collected Papers*, The Hague, Nijhoff.

Screaton-Page, G. (1971), 'Social Nudism: The Social Organisation of Southern Ontario Nudist Camps' in Mann, W. E. (ed) *Social Deviance in Canada*, Toronto, Copp Gek Publishing.

Weinburg, S. W. (1967), 'The Nudist Camp: Way of Life and Social Structure' in *Human Organisation*, Vol. 26, No 3 pp91-9.

Weinburg, S. W. (1968), 'Becoming a Nudist', in Rubington E. and Weinburg, S. (eds) *Deviance: The Interactionist Perspective*, Canada, Macmillan.

Weinburg, S. W. (1970), 'Sexual Modesty, Social Meanings and the Nudist Camp' in Douglas, J. (ed) *Observations of Deviance*, New York, Random House.

Weinburg, S. W. (1970), 'The Nudist Management of Respectability: Strategy for and Consequences of the Construction of a Situated Morality', in Douglas, J. E. (ed.) *Deviance and Respectability*, New York, Basic Books, pp375-404.

Wyness, M. (1994), 'Keeping Tabs on an Uncivil Society', *Sociology* Vol. 28 no 1 pp193-209.

6 'Safe'? Involving children in child protection

Ian Butler with Howard Williamson

Introduction

This chapter explores how child protection procedures and social work practice should alter in order to reflect children's own accounts of the experience of abuse and of the kind of help children and young people find most useful. It is based on the findings of a study of 200 children and young people, aged between 6 and 17 (Butler and Williamson 1994).

Child abuse and child protection

It is commonplace to assert that child abuse (and therefore child protection) is a negotiated process (Parton 1991, Archard 1993, Corby 1993). There are few absolutes as, culturally and temporally, child abuse is continuously defined and re-defined. The broader socio-historical context within which harms inflicted upon children take place is routinely invoked (see Rogers, Hevey and Ash 1989), to establish some sense of the infinite perfectibility of our understanding of child abuse and our responses to it. It is generally accepted therefore, that child abuse and child protection cannot be accounted for or understood without reference to the way in which we account for and respond to children generally.

This is not the occasion to rehearse the whole post-Aries (Aries 1960) thesis concerning the social construction of childhood, but it is our contention that the contemporary, culturally dominant construction of childhood is inimical to any serious development of the kind of child protective mechanisms that directly reflect the experience of children themselves. We have argued elsewhere in this volume that contemporary accounts of childhood constitute a deficit model, whereby, children are defined primarily on the basis of their dependence in order to satisfy the unmet needs of adults.

Childhood, we argue, is widely conceived of as a state of incompetence relative to adulthood. To be a child is to be not yet an adult nor to possess the intellectual, emotional and physical capacities to act autonomously. The naturalistic foundation of such a construction is the developmental psychology of Freud and Piaget. In both cases, adulthood is the desirable end-point of childhood and each successive stage in the development of the 'less than adult' is not simply a quantitative advance but a qualitative improvement upon that which went before, until the consummation of the process is achieved in adulthood. By this reading, adulthood is a settled state of being and childhood merely a process. This process is driven by a fury of evolutionary, biological and hormonal imperatives until the advent of the staid, 'middle-aged individual of modest, moderate and settled needs' (Hart on J.S. Mill).

One cannot doubt the fact of human growth and development (although the several facts are arguable) but we do draw attention once more to the unnecessary but pervasive assumption that childhood is not simply quantitatively and qualitatively different from adulthood (which is simply to state the obvious) but more damagingly, that it is also, *by its very nature*, inferior. It is not simply a matter of relative competence but also a matter of the cultural presumption of the subordinate status of childhood and the relative powerlessness of children to which we draw attention.

Both of these factors are probably implicated in any explanation of the phenomenon of abuse itself. It is the argument of this chapter that such a construction of childhood has also had profound effects on the process and structures of child protective services in the UK. This is to suggest that 'child protection', in the sense of social work policy and practice, like most other services to children, has developed without direct reference to the prime objects of the exercise, children themselves.

Involving children in child protection

Were it not for the cultural presumption of the relative worthlessness of childhood experience in itself (as opposed to its value as preparation for adulthood), the question of involving children in the process of their own protection either would not arise or else would be a relatively simple one about age and competence. Despite the rhetoric of 'partnership', 'empowerment' and 'user involvement' (Buchanan 1994, Cloke & Davies 1995) which might have talismanic qualities for practitioners but only expressive value for young clients, children are routinely excluded from child protection work. With apologies to Arnstein (1972), who recognised early the potential for participative approaches to mask the oppressive effects of social work practice, one can conceive of a model of children's involvement in child protection as follows (Figure 6:1):

Non-participation

this is the passive kind of non-participation where a child is simply ignored. It should be difficult to imagine such a situation but in our experience, the bulk of child protection work is accounted for by scrupulous attention to the behaviour of adults and a complete disregard for the consequences of that behaviour for children (Reder, Duncan & Gray 1993). One need only contrast the investment of material and human resources in a criminal prosecution to the investment made in post-abuse services.

Manipulation

this is where a child is *only* required for forensic or evidential purposes or simply for administrative convenience to play a part in the process. The aims and outcomes of the process are quite separate from the needs and wishes of the child but the child's involvement is required in order to facilitate the process. Involvement at this point means turning up for medicals, preparing witness statements, moving placements etc.. One might consider the SSI Report on the use of video evidence in this respect (DOH 1994) which found that only 6% of the 14,000 filmed interviews with child witnesses carried out in 1993 had been used in court. This may reflect more upon the criminal justice system than the practices of social workers, of course.

Therapeutic terrorism

this is where the child is 'social worked over' as part of an absolute requirement for them to recover. This may have a lot to do with adults' need to 'make things better'. For example, whilst attending a conference on substitute family care in the US, we were presented with what we can only describe as forms of ritualised child abuse. In the name of a variety of therapeutic imperatives, children and young people were subjected to sustained and intensive emotional working over, most of this on video tape. Children as young as three or four were left in great sobbing heaps as some off screen voice intoned them to 'really get in touch with their pain' or to 'face the reality of their situation'. The distress of the children did not register at all. Therapist knew best. We objected not only to the exploitation of these children for the purposes of the conference but also to the process itself. We received very short shrift and were accused of being too emotionally involved with the case material - note 'case material', not children. This case material was there to be formed in the image of the therapist. The children would be cured when they conformed to the particular therapeutic regime. What happened en route was unfortunate possibly, but necessary, certainly. All means, to the zealot, justify the ends.

Information giving

this is a form of tokenism where a child is told what may happen to them but not given any real choice. Involvement here often takes the form of 'working agreements' or 'contracts' which contain lots of things that the child must do, a few that the social worker might try, sanctions for the child and absolution for the social worker (See Atherton and Dowling 1989).

Information exchange

this is where the co-operation begins and the involvement of the child might just make a difference. The child's views (the magical 'ascertainable wishes and feelings' of the Children Act 1989) are beginning to be heard and transmitted in case conference minutes, review forms and court reports. They are collected, a little like stamps, for ritual purposes of doing the social work by the book, but the fact that the child is heard does create the opportunity that what is said might occasionally be valued.

Collaboration/partnership

never has there been an idea in social work open to such a wide range of applications in practice as this. In this instance, the reference is to a partnership with the child not necessarily its carers. Involvement here means that what the child says, is acted upon, at least in so far as it is permitted to alter the opinions and judgements of the adults involved. The child is involved not just for the expressive value of involvement - because it makes him or her feel good - but because of its instrumental value - things will happen *because* the child is involved.

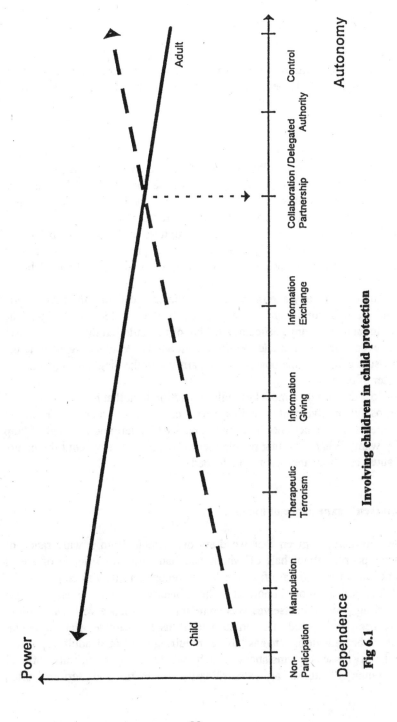

Fig 6.1 Involving children in child protection

Delegated authority

involvement here means that the child is controlling some of what is happening and, with the active support and advice of a social worker other trusted individual, is being fully consulted on those matters that remain outside of his or her control.

Control

the New Jerusalem. Involvement is wholly on the child's terms and we should be talking about the involvement of the social worker. This is what we say we aim for in work with adults. There is another form of control that a child can take of the child protection process and that is active non-participation whereby either through disruptive, unco-operative behaviour or simple inactivity, the child ensures that the process grinds to a halt or passes them by untouched. This is the form of control usually available to children.

Any child of any age or level of competence can find themself at any point on this continuum, usually towards the far left hand side. The determinant is not any particular attribute of the child but the relative power over events of the child and the significant adults. Whether this is quite the zero-sum game that the position of the arrows on the diagram suggests, is a matter of opinion.

How then might a model of child protection look that had the active and purposeful involvement of children as a central goal and which reflected children's own experience and their capacity to determine the kind of help they want? What do young people themselves have to say about the nature of abuse and how they want to be helped?

Children's experience of harm

Not surprisingly, given that we drew our sample from a wide range of young people, about half of whom had had direct experience of social work, the variety of harmful experiences reported to us was equally wide. What is perhaps more important is the subjective meaning given to events by young people themselves was sometimes at variance with what might have been anticipated. This in turn leads us to examine what particular 'harms' become designated as 'abuse' requiring an official, adult response.

Even those circumstances which would register on any official continuum of abuse as extraordinarily traumatic and serious, often contained meanings for the child that might not have been obvious to the casual, social work observer. A particularly striking example is that of the 16-year old young woman who had been raped by her step-brother at the age of 11:

> Interv.
> So presumably being raped was the worst thing that has ever happened to you?
>
> Resp.
> It was bad, but not the worst. The worst was when my step-brother held me still - he used to get extra pocket money off my dad for helping him hit me - and then my dad broke all my fingers, one by one ...

Similarly, a 15 year old girl told us:

> I used to live with my nan. When I was just turned 14 I was raped by strangers. The police took me home and nan said she don't want me here any more. That's why I came into a home ... But that wasn't really the worst thing. That could happen to anybody. It just happened to be me. The worst thing was when my dad hit me for no reason. I never understood it. He was my *dad*.

In similarly extreme circumstances, one young person, who at age 9 had witnessed the murder of her mother by her father, reported the real trauma to be the lack of information and explanation available at the time:

> I never saw my mum in hospital after my dad attacked her. I didn't go to the funeral. I don't even know now where her grave is. Nobody told me anything, probably because they thought I was too young. But nobody even tried. And I can't ask now 'cos all the staff who were here then have moved on. But that was actually worse than my mum actually dying...
>
> (girl, 17)

Even in less dramatic, but no less traumatic, bereavements, lack of information about the most momentous events in one's life was an additional source of pain:

It was when my dad died, after six years of leukaemia. No-one had told me how bad he was. It was a big shock. I cried a lot.

(girl, 14)

The depth and duration of the hurt suffered by children may also be obscured by an adult belief that children 'will get over it'. Long after the abuse stops, the hurt can continue:

I still have nightmares. Something happened to me when I was six. It was a friend of the family who used to baby-sit for us. My mum says not to worry, 'he won't come back'. But I still worry. In my dreams, he still comes back.

(girl, 11)

Children experience other forms of adult behaviour as intensely hurtful, particularly familial arguments and domestic violence:

I can hear my parents arguing when I'm lying in bed at night. Sometimes they're arguing about me. I can't sleep and I can't stop worrying. Quite often I'm afraid to go down in the morning.

(girl, 14)

The worst thing is the arguments between my mum and her new boyfriend. He's horrible. He's nasty - he's always teasing me. I talk to my nan and grandad and then they have arguments with my mum. My dad says 'don't worry about it', but it's horrible. It goes on all the time.

(girl, 10)

When my parents had a fight, dad hit mum and gave her a black eye. He left, but he's back now.

(boy, 10)

My dad used to hit me and my mum, so we moved away. Then I went to stay with my dad and I wanted to stay with him. So my mum rejected me and vanished. I didn't know where she was. It was horrible. But it was brilliant with my dad. Now he's got a new girlfriend and it's all gone bad. He hits me, keeps me in, cuts off my money. I hate him. I want to go, but I've got no-where to go. I don't want to go home at night.

(girl, 14)

It is doubtful if adults would be prepared to acknowledge their own arguments or their violence directed to each other as actually or potentially harmful or abusive. They certainly hurt children.

But it was the routine catalogue of harm suffered by children at the hands of other children that most readily challenges adult conceptions of what constitutes abuse. Bullying enters and damages the lives of most children:

Older kids are always pushing me around, piss-taking, laughing at me. I don't know why. I haven't done anything to them. Every day when I have to go to school, I get frightened that they're going to pick on me again today. I just try and hide and hope they don't see me.

(boy, 12)

The bullying at school can be really nasty. Sometimes, just before break time, I start to shake in class because I'm so scared about going outside.

(girl, 13)

The worst thing is at school when you go out into the playground. The older kids come over and take your bag off you and chuck it around, or nick your hat and won't let you have it back. You get really upset, 'cos they're all laughing at you and you look stupid in front of your mates.

(boy, 12)

Because I'm quite good at school, I get picked on by the other girls who call me a 'snob' and poke and push me around. Sometimes I don't really care, but I must admit I do find it hard to fit in and that gets to me sometimes.

(girl, 14)

Elsewhere in this volume (see Pugsley, Coffey and Delamont) the capacity of children to offer resistance through ritual is described. One would hope that adults might be prepared to offer more than symbolic help.

In commenting on our findings, we have noted elsewhere that,

Only by listening to the *meaning* imputed to such experiences by the young people concerned can those seeking to support them secure a measure of understanding of how they are affecting them. An expanded awareness of what actually troubles children and young people may lead to a more sensitive and appropriate response to particular individuals. Name calling, for example, does hurt. It might not hurt an adult to the same degree (possibly) and the hurt is not as serious as the potential hurt caused by other forms of abuse towards children. However, to deny the pain it *can* cause in the face of what children and young people actually say is to demean children, disregard the validity of their accounts, and thereby perpetuate the communication gap that not only exists, but appears to be growing, between children and adults.

(Butler and Williamson 1994: 64)

Listening

Our larger study dealt at some length with the fact that many young people had already lost faith in adults' capacity to help them deal with their problems to the degree that they had entirely given up on them (See also Rees 1993). Some of the reasons given by these children, based on their experiences of adults' reactions, were very widely shared.

Many of the children who spoke to us could find no reason to discriminate between the lack of understanding displayed by what we called 'adult professionals' (e.g. social workers, teachers, doctors etc.) and 'professional adults' who were just full time 'grown ups' (e.g. parents).

Re: social workers

They do one good thing for you and two things bad. You don't know where you stand. They go on about knowing what's best for you, but it's all out of books. How can they know your 'best interests' when they don't even know you? What kind of contact do social workers have with their kids? One visit in two or three months? Nothing at all. I know they're trying to do their best for you. But they haven't been what you've been through. So they'll never know, they'll never understand.

(girl, 14)

They talk to you and try to get round your problems but they
don't understand. They don't know nothing about what it's
really like for you.

(boy, 15)

Re: parents

They don't listen. You can't get through to them. Times
have changed since they were young but they see things like
it was then. They don't understand what things are like
now... No-one's on our side.

(girl, 15)

Parents ignore you. They don't show any interest in you and
then they blame you when things go wrong.

(girl, 12)

The direct consequence of a lack of basic sensitivity or interest is the
imposition by adults of their own views.

Re: social workers

They don't really listen. And then they don't believe you.
My mum is mentally disturbed. And because I wouldn't talk
to them - I mean, I've always kept people at a distance, that's
just the way I am - they thought I was disturbed, like mum.
When I told them about being raped, they put it down to my
imagination. Why should I imagine that? But he's owned
up now. But no-one believed me. Social workers don't
listen. They see what they want to see. They don't want to
know.

(girl, 17)

Re: parents

I had this fight at school and got sent home. It was the first
time I'd ever had a fight and I was really upset. Dad wasn't
bothered at first - he said talk to mum. Then he came in and
said 'Did you win?'... Adults don't understand kids' reasons,
they don't hear their explanations - kids don't win. It's bad
for both of you, but somehow you both end up fighting at
the time. He's my mate. But I couldn't get a word in
edgeways. My dad only wanted to know bits of the story -

the bits he'd understand. He's stubborn. He didn't want to listen. And when he'd heard what he wanted to hear, he changed the subject. He didn't want to listen to what I wanted to say.

(boy, 13)

Misunderstanding was often closely followed by other inappropriate reactions. Adults trivialise what it is that is bothering children.

People treat you as a joke. They don't take you seriously.

(boy, 13)

Parents don't take things seriously. They just tell you to grow up.

(girl, 14)

Mums are a bit more understanding. Dads just treat things as a laugh. They won't admit to their experiences, but I bet they had the same worries when they were kids. So they just joke about things that we want them to treat seriously.

(boy, 12)

I wouldn't talk to the staff here. They don't treat me seriously. And I don't trust social workers. Just because I put on a friendly, smiley face they don't realise I want them to be serious with me.

(boy, 12)

Sometimes they take you seriously but a lot of the time they just laugh at you.

(boy, 9)

For other young people who spoke to us, the response they received from adults would swing suddenly from trivialising (epitomised by the expression 'why don't you grow up?') to overreaction and the adoption of an over-protective and disempowering stance.

Adults keep on joking about it but sometimes they suddenly realise it is serious and then they go over the top.

(girl, 10)

If you tell your teacher or your parents you are getting picked on by other kids, they go in head first and that makes things worse. When I told my dad I was being bullied, he came steaming down to the school and the teacher had a go at these kids. But they just picked on me worse 'cos they thought it was a laugh that I'd had to tell my dad.

(boy, 13)

When my mum and dad was fighting I talked to my nan about it. I didn't want her to do anything. I just wanted to tell someone and I'd always got on with my nan. But she went and had a go at my mum for upsetting me and then my mum had a go at me for telling nan which she says I shouldn't have done. So it made everything worse. I think nan got the wrong impression. She didn't really understand.

(girl, 9)

The worst form of over-reaction by adults is when it is perceived to rebound on children themselves and a process begins which, in essence, is about 'blaming the victim'.

Me and my friends always used to hang around in the park. One day there was this man there. He wasn't doing anything but he spooked me. He was there every day for about a week. So I told my mum. I got grounded for a month! It was like it was my fault. I wish I hadn't told her now.

(girl, 14)

The greatest source of doubt concerning the capacity of adults to help children effectively arose from young people's fears over possible breaches of confidentiality. Perhaps more social work angst has been devoted to this subject than any other. Nonetheless, the young people who spoke to us are not convinced.

Some young people had developed strategies to test the water. One 14-year old girl, when asked from whom she might seek support, said,

I suppose I might ask for advice from social workers or a teacher, but you don't know who they'd tell. I'd probably test them out with small things and see how fast other people found out.

A 10-year old girl, presented with a similar question, commented,

I'd be too scared to. You don't know them. You don't know whether they're going to cheat on you.

A widely held belief amongst children and young people is that professionals have an enormous capacity for 'gossip'.

Sometimes social workers tell you personal things about themselves. I think they're trying to get you to trust them. But are they true? How do you know? And then they say things like 'Can you keep a secret?' and you think this is because they want you to tell them your secrets. If they're telling me secrets, they'll probably tell mine to somebody else. They're loudmouths.

(girl, 11)

Finally, an ironic commentary on the issue of confidentiality was provided by young people themselves. The following exchange took place in a group interview with teenage girls:

- I'd talk to Miss _____ (teacher). She's got her head screwed on. She's caring and she'd be confidential about it.

- And she's got her own problems which she told in confidence to some of the students in the sixth form.

- Yeah, and THEY told the whole school!

Helping

Children and young people gave the following three reasons for approaching adults or peers to talk about their problems:

- to unload
- to elicit ideas and possible choices for action
- to catalyse action by others

In our experience, young people are only too aware that, ultimately, it is *they* who are most likely to bring about the resolution to their problems. Thus the first two reasons are by far the most important ones to children and young people themselves. Young people do not seek or expect action by others *unless they ask for it*. Broadly, they seek to *unload* problems on friends and seek *advice, information and guidance* from adults. Younger children are more likely to believe and hope that others can 'sort things out' on their behalf, but even the 8/9-year olds we interviewed still felt that they had to take most of the initiative on those matters which concerned them most. As we have noted elsewhere (Butler and Williamson 1994, p82):

> The dilemma for children and young people, as they see it, is that once they convey something to adults, the power to determine what should then be done is - too often - taken out of their hands.

This point also needs to be considered in relation to what young people told us about their trust in adults to maintain confidentiality. Without experience of reliable assurances of confidentiality, many children and young people do not trust adults sufficiently to confide in them. If children and young people do not trust adults in this way, they will, as we have recorded, talk to no-one. In this case, what confidence should we have in our current models of child protection services? How can we protect children who can not talk to us (See Gilkes 1989) or, if they do, who feel powerless to control what happens next?

So what are children looking for in the help that adults can offer?

Young people want individualised attention, careful listening, without trivialising or being dismissive of the issues raised:

> A good listener. Someone who doesn't immediately get back at you with 'oh, you're tired, you'll be all right tomorrow' - that's not listening.
>
> (girl, 11)

One young man, reflecting on his experience of being taken into care, commented,

> All I ever got was a pat on the head. Nobody ever spoke to me about it - and I'm not one to go to somebody and talk about it. Professionals need to emphasise their willingness to listen and try to understand. If they're willing to listen, I'm willing to tell.
>
> (boy, 17)

This particular young man was poignantly articulate on the quality of explanation offered to him by his professional carers:

> They said I was too young, that I wouldn't understand. But they never even tried. I was young, but they failed to notice that I was trying to understand. They did things to me - where I lived, where I went to school, the clothes I wore. I always wanted to know why. Why did I have to move homes, why did I have to change schools?
>
> All they kept saying to me was that I'd be a 'bright young man' and I'd understand when I was older. What a stupid thing to say. If they thought I was bright, even more so, they should have heard me asking to be told why all this was happening to me. If people refuse to listen and don't even try to explain, it all means nothing. They should have shown more confidence in me, instead of undermining it.

His regret at being prevented from being the author of his own biography was echoed by many children and young people who looked for a non-judgmental and non-directive response from adults:

> People offer you support and help but you should always be able to do something different if you want to or if you think it won't work. You don't want to feel you've got to do what they say.
>
> (boy, 10)

> I want my own choices - otherwise my life might be ruined by someone else's mistakes.
>
> (girl, 12)

> Instead of saying 'you have to do this', say 'why don't you try this and if you don't like it, don't bother'. People who look at things from your point of view, who take time to find out what you're thinking is best for you.
>
> (boy, 14)

> I think everybody needs advice from time to time but not from people who talk down to you. They should give you choices: 'This is what I'd do, but it's up to you'.
>
> (girl, 14)

If you're given advice, it should be 'maybe', not 'you must' and they should tell you better why they think something is a good idea.

(girl, 10)

Children recognise early that life is the art of the possible and value honesty and 'straight talking' in the adults around them.

Re: teacher

She's prepared to listen to you and she talks straight, not always what you want to hear. But it usually makes sense.

(girl, 15)

Re: residential social worker

Everybody complains about her but there's no-one better than her for listening and coming up with good ideas. You don't like admitting it, but she's usually right in the end.

(girl, 17)

Re: field social worker

Interv.
So what have you made of the social workers you've had?

Resp.
Some have been all right, some have been crap.

Interv.
What's been the difference?

Resp.
The good ones have been kind to me. They do things quickly once they say they'll do something. They understand how you act and know what's on your mind....

Interv.
And the bad ones?

101

Resp.

Oh, they never get things done, they're always making promises they never keep.

'Safe'?

'Safe' is a word that many children use to mean that someone can be trusted, is reliable, is a friend.

The essential question is whether the adult world wants to assist children who are suffering harm in feeling 'safe' (as *children* define it) or to ensure that children appear to be 'protected' (as adults define it). The former demands flexible, sensitive interventions along the lines of those described by the children whose voices we have recorded in this chapter. These will require adults to respect and keep the confidence and confidentiality of children and young people to a far greater extent than they are used to doing; it will require adults to countenance much more self determination by children and young people which may be experienced as taking even greater risks; it will require greater trust and faith than either party would currently seem to have in and for the other. The latter form of intervention calls for rigid procedures imposed from above in response to political and professional imperatives, where it is the adult who feels safe from the uncertainties of an uncertain world and the hostility of an unforgiving public and press. The latter may satisfy the 'social conscience' but only the former can enable children and young people to equip themselves with the resources to deal with the social realities they currently encounter or expect to encounter in the future. It is therefore *this* task which should provide the driving force for social work endeavour, underpinned by the value-base of meeting individual needs; for without such a value-base, social work practice is vulnerable to blowing around in the political wind (Lorenz 1993) with no anchor point to ensure it is grounded in the real lives and hopes of those it seeks to serve.

With the help of colleagues (Hopkins 1994) we have devised some broad principles for effective child protection practice that really does seek to involve children and young people:

Involvement in what?

- When working with children who have experienced abuse, it is vitally necessary to establish what children themselves see as the primary causes of pain, distress and fear.

- Children's perceptions and fears, as well as acknowledged traumatic events, can have a significant impact on children's lives and well-being and these need to be addressed and validated at all stages of investigation, assessment and therapeutic work.

- Child care practitioners should actively address the consequences and associated difficulties resulting from traumatic events experienced by children and pay special attention to the effects of those actions taken specifically to protect the child.

Involvement with whom?

- Children should always be consulted, as part of the negotiation and review of work, to identify any preference they may have regarding the gender, race and culture of their worker.

- Children should always be consulted, as a formal part of any individual programme of work, on their choice of a 'safe' or 'trusted person' to support them.

- In allocating and planning work, priority should be given to ensuring continuity of key practitioners/trusted persons.

Involvement on whose terms?

- When receiving information from children about their concerns, practitioners/workers should make quite sure that they understand why children are sharing the information and what form of help they require.

- Working agreements with young people should ensure that they retain maximum possible choice/autonomy within the working relationship, while having easy access to advice and support outside of it.

- Upon receipt of information from a child about her/himself, practitioners/workers should always consult the young person about their mandate to take action and about the form and content of any such action.

- Clear and understandable 'confidentiality contracts' should form part of all work agreements and reviews.

Involvement to what extent?

- In planning work, children should understand and be involved in setting objectives/timescales which should be realistic, achievable and have meaning/relevance for the young person.

- Work plans/agreements should include a section dedicated to individual children's definition of their problems and the effects that these are having on them.

- Practitioners/trusted persons should have the ability to listen to and understand what individual children require and have the skills to design specific programmes of work to meet their different needs.

- Practitioners/trusted persons should ensure that children are aware of/understand the options available to them during the professional's or other adult's involvement with them.

- Practitioners/trusted persons will provide children with information about services that is relevant to their needs, readily understandable and factually correct.

- Children's perception about the reliability and effectiveness of services/service providers should be recorded and addressed in service evaluation and practice supervision.

On the basis of these principles, we believe that young people's idea of 'safe' can be allied with the adult notion of 'protection' to the mutual advantage of both. Neither children nor adults have a monopoly on wisdom in this area. Adults might do well to remember that.

In the context of the larger themes of this book, observing and analysing the social phenomenon of child abuse, from a *child's standpoint* (see chapters 1 and 2), which begins by listening to their accounts, does open up the possibility of a significant new understanding of key aspects of inter-generational relations. For example, the dominant, adult construction of abuse itself reflects the differential capacity to define one's own experience, especially as a child. Successive re-negotiations of abuse similarly provide a marker for the historical development of the balance of power between children and adults to act in society and to construct social 'truths' about it. Similar points could be made in relation to the way in which therapeutic or other 'protective' regimes serve the various interests of adult and child participants differentially. And each avenue of enquiry may tell us something more about the way in which social relations of other sorts are ordered.

Listen, we might all learn something.

References

Archard, D. (1993), *Children - Rights and Childhood*, London: Routledge.

Aries, P. (1960), *L'Enfant et la vie familiale sous l'ancien regime*, Paris: Libraire Plon, Translated by Robert Baldick as 'Centuries of Childhood' (1962) London: Jonathan Cape.

Arnstein, R. (1972), 'Power to the people: An assessment of the community action and model cities experience', *Public Administration Review*, Vol. 32.

Atherton, C and P. Dowling (1989), 'Using written agreements: the family's point of view', in J. Aldgate (ed.), *Using Written Agreements with Children and Families*, London. Family Rights Group.

Buchanan, A. (1994) *Partnership in Practice*, Aldershot. Avebury.

Butler, I. and Williamson, H. (1994), *Children Speak: Children, Trauma and Social Work*, London. Longman.

Cloke, C. and Davies, M. (1995), *Participation and Empowerment in Child Protection*, London. Pitman.

Corby, B. (1993), *Child Abuse - Towards a Knowledge Base*, Buckingham. OUP.

Gilkes, J. (1989), 'Coming to terms with sexual abuse: a day care perspective', in P. Riches (ed.), *Responses to Cleveland: Improving Services for Child Sexual Abuse*, London. Whiting and Birch/National Children's Bureau.

Hopkins, N. (1994), 'Safe'? in Butler, I. and Williamson, H. (1994), *Children Speak: Children, Trauma and Social Work*, London. Longman.

Lorenz, W. (1993), *Social Work in a Changing Europe*, London. Routledge.

Parton, N. (1991), *Governing the Family: Child Care, Child Protection and the State*, Basingstoke. Macmillan.

Reder, P., Duncan, S. and Gray, M. (1993), *Beyond Blame - Child Abuse Tragedies Revisited*, London. RKP.

Rees, G. (1993), *Hidden Truths: Young People's experience of running away*, London. The Children's Society.

Rogers, W., Hevey, D. and Ash, E. (eds) (1989), *Child Abuse and Neglect: Facing the Challenge*, London. Batsford.

7 Whose life is it anyway?

Anne Crowley

This chapter considers the role of qualitative research in seeking to understand how notions of participation are understood and experienced by children and young people. Examining the particular situation of children and young people who are 'looked after' by local authorities, the author argues that we must appreciate the world of 'adult decision making' as experienced by children and young people if we are to successfully implement strategies designed to increase young people's active participation in decision making. The importance of listening to children's own accounts will be emphasised with reference to the deficiencies of service responses based on what adult professionals *think* will lead to increased participation by children and people, rather than responses based on children's own accounts of 'what works' and 'doesn't work' for them. Consideration is given to the particular methodological and ethical issues that arise when adults undertake research with children.

Learning to make well informed choices is recognised as an important aspect of growing up. The ability to collect information, to sift it and to take decisions for better or for worse is an important marker of 'adulthood' (Gardner, 1987), yet our social institutions rarely afford children and young people consistent opportunities to be consulted about decisions which affect their lives. Others (Archard, 1993; Butler and Williamson, 1994) have attested to the way in which childhood is usually constructed by adults on a 'deficit model' whereby, in order to meet the needs of adults, children are maintained as a seperate and subordinate social group in contempory British Society. For example, adults are seen as the real consumers, even of children's services, from education to child health (Alderson, 1995).

It is important to remember this in any consideration of participation in decision making processes. As a review of the literature makes it evident, the balance of power is a crucial determinant of effective participation. As Stein (1983) notes, typologies of participation are characterised by different degrees of power sharing and unless consumers have real power within organisations, listening and involvement may mean very little real action and change on the part of those in authority. Hodgson (1988), in his review of empirical research that questions the significance of participation by 'looked after' children and young people, concludes that participation in this context is about influencing the balance of power in decision making:

> Participation ... can be defined as the process by which influence is knowingly exercised by individuals or groups over events or decisions which significantly affect them.
>
> (1988: 20)

Children in our society are generally propertyless, economically inactive individuals and the democratic structures of our society give little power to people in such a position. As Shaw comments:

> Children occupy a position of legal, economic, social and personal dependence from which they can escape only gradually by growing older. Attempts to escape ahead of time bring them into conflict with parents and a variety of external agencies.
>
> (1989 :3)

The potential for conflict exists, despite moves in recent years in legislative and policy terms, towards involving children and young people in decision making. The Gillick Judgement (Gillick v West Norfolk and Wisbech Area Health Authority, 1986. A.C. 112) for the first time linked a child's right to choose to the child's intelligence and maturity. In the course of the judgement, Lord Denning was quoted as saying (in Hewer vs. Bryant, 1970) that parents had:

> a dwindling right which the courts will hesitate to enforce against the wishes of the child and the more so the older he is. It starts with the right of control and ends with little more than advice.

The U.N. Convention on the Rights of the Child, the international human rights agreement setting minimum standards for the care and protection of children and young people, was ratified by the U.K. Government in December 1991. Article 12 of the Convention states that children and young people must be allowed to say what they think when adults are making decisions or taking action which affects them. Their views must also be taken into account, depending on their age and maturity.

Specifically, the Convention states, that children have a right to be heard when courts or official bodies are making decisions which will affect them.

The Children Act 1989 provides a number of opportunities for promoting the rights of children to be consulted, ensuring they have a voice in decisions affecting their lives and allowing for consumer views to inform service planning and delivery. In the wake of scandals in the late eighties, which highlighted the abuse children suffered at the hands of adults (London Borough of Brent (1985), London Borough of Greenwich (1987), London Borough of Lambeth (1987), Cleveland (1988)), The Children Act set out to reform child care law. The Act aimed to strike a balance between the rights of children to express their views on decisions made about their lives, the rights of parents to exercise their responsibilities towards the child and the duty of the state to intervene where the child's welfare requires it.

Despite this apparent emphasis in law and policy on the rights of children and young people to participate in decision making affecting their lives, there has been little monitoring of the impact of such changes. Research into the extent to which children and young people are able to participate in decision making and the impact of policy and practice initiatives designed to improve levels of participation have received little attention from researchers.

This void is particularly disconcerting when we consider how dependent children and young people are on adults to enforce their 'right' to participate. As Shaw (1989) suggests, the notion of rights in relation to children is not so much a reality as an easy slogan or at best an aspiration. Adults have legal rights which, if infringed, can be enforced by legal action against some person or organisation. Children's rights are generally not of this kind, essentially but are defined and enforced by adults on the child's behalf.

Children's dependency on adults to define and enforce their rights is not unproblematic, as Gardner (1987) concludes:

> We live in a society that is alive to the claims of consumer and pressure groups. To a large extent the battle to establish that an adult's rights and wishes have inherent value, a battle has been won, and part of the victory has benefited children. However children are particularly vulnerable in that they are overwhelmingly the innocent recipients of what other people think, and they have trailed on the coat tails of their elders.
>
> (1987: 103)

Until recently, research into the child care system itself has commonly not focused on the child's experience. As Alderson concludes:

> Most research directly on children is devoted to measuring them, using a model of animal research to measure their growth, disease and behaviour.

(1995: 40)

Evidence about children is largely drawn from replies by teachers, parents, social workers and other adults. Only two of the nine, DHSS-funded, larger scale, research studies on social work decisions in child care, gave an account of the views of children and young people themselves (Rowe, 1984; Fisher, 1986). These studies clearly noted that a comparison of the views of parents, social workers and the children themselves showed clear discrepancies. They re-enforce the importance of gaining children's own accounts of their experiences rather than just the bald facts of their case histories or the perceptions of professionals and parents. Packman *et al* (1986) who conducted a large scale study of how and why decisions are made about taking children into care and the effects of these decisions concluded:

> the children in question - the ultimate consumers of the service on offer - were the group least likely to be consulted, and there were discussions with less that 1 in 10 before adult minds were made up.

(1986: 79)

Reasons are sometimes given as to why children's views are not sought - 'it's too lengthy a process'; 'children were too young to be interviewed'; 'possible breaches of confidentiality'. Millham *et al* (1986) studied the child care system and the problems of maintaining links between children in care and their parents. They suggested that often the age of children made it inappropriate for them to explore the children's own accounts. Instead reliance is made on the perceptions of parents, carers and health professionals and their own observations.

There should be no doubt that qualitative research with children and young people brings particular methodological and ethical issues that can be difficult and time-consuming. Undertaking rigorous research with data that can be considered as reliable and valid in a manner which is also respectful and sympathetic to children presents many challenges for social researchers. The development of qualitative research with children has clearly been hindered by the hitherto limited debate on the ethical and methodological considerations of interviewing children or involving children more broadly in social research. The Code of Ethics of the British Sociological Association makes no specific reference to children and young people.

More recently, Alderson (1995) has examined the ethical issues involved in social research with children. She reviews ethical standards and guidance and suggests practical ways of applying them throughout the research process. Her work is timely and valuable. Researchers should feel more confident about involving young people in research if they are able to observe high standards and take moral dilemmas seriously.

My own experience of conducting qualitative research with children highlights some of the dilemmas and challenges facing social researchers. It gives one example of how children's own accounts of their experiences can be used positively to inform the transformation of 'principles' into 'action' in a manner that children themselves are more likely to be able to discern and to which they can relate. Moreover, whilst a small scale study of young people's own accounts of decision making processes cannot be seen to represent the experiences and views of 'young people' or indeed 'children', this study highlights the importance of gaining young people's views as to how they (as individuals) can be assisted to participate more fully in decision making processes. Routinely evaluating decision making processes with reference to the young person's own experiences of these processes should be a significant element of any strategy designed to increase participation by young people. Over time, as more data is collated, the influences of race, gender, age and other variables will become more apparent.

The account of the research presented here, also seeks to demonstrate that the *particular* dilemmas and experiences of conducting social research with children need to be treated as problematic, for they tell us a lot about the *modus operandi* of interaction between the respective worlds of professional adults and disadvantaged children. As Alderson argues:

> When there are discrepancies in power, such as between
> children and adults, it is not possible to be neutral; research
> either re-enforces the unequal status quo or questions it.
>
> (1995: 42)

The research was commissioned by The Children's Society, in order to identify levels of 'participation' by 'looked after' children and young people, prior to the development of a service aimed at increasing participation in decision making processes in one local authority. The Children's Society proposed to undertake a study aimed at identifying the existing levels of 'participation' by children and young people eligible to use the new service. In considering how such a study should proceed it became immediately obvious that participation is not an easy concept to define and measure. The multidimensional nature of the concept of study thus ruled out any large scale measurement of the incidence of participation without first undertaking a more qualitative exploration of the concept itself.

Previous studies concerned with participation by 'looked after' children and young people (Page and Clark, 1977; Gardner, 1987; Hodgson, 1988) identified the need to meet, listen and take seriously the views of children and young people. In the absence of any 'adult led' initiatives to acknowledge and consider the actual views of children and young people who were the recipients of 'care' services, it was young people themselves who pushed their actual views and experiences up the agenda. In 1975, the National Children's Bureau hosted the first ever conference of children in care. There followed a series of meetings and a publication, *'Who Cares?'* which reproduced young people's views unaltered by adults. *'Who Cares?'* became a catalyst for a long campaign to make local authority care more responsive to the wishes and feelings of young people. The stark reality of young people's lack of involvement in decision making was illustrated by one young person:

> I had one social worker and he tried to get me lots of foster homes but he always done it his way, pretending it was me who was thinking it out. But I always knew it was him. What I thought or felt about the foster parents just didn't matter ... sometimes I wonder what social workers are really employed for, to think with us or to think for us.

(1977: 15)

The formation of The National Association for Young People in Care (NAYPIC) focused a campaign for children and young people in care to have a say in decision making that affects their lives. The organisation, run by young people presently or previously in care, conducted a postal survey on young people's experiences of child care reviews (Stein and Ellis, 1983). Review meetings represent the key decision making forum concerned with planning for children and young people who are looked after. Local authorities are required to formally review plans at regular intervals and young people themselves are expected to participate in the process.

NAYPIC received responses from 465 young people which indicated that most young people wanted to attend their reviews. They found that one third of young people in children's homes and one quarter of those in foster homes had not attended a review, some didn't even know what a review was.

For the purpose of our study a more exploratory approach was required. Participation, in the context of decision making and looked after children and young people, can best be understood not as a principle but as a process (Hodgson, 1988).

To gain an understanding of the nature and level of participation by young people in one local authority, our research design employed in depth interviews with 'looked after' young people. This was felt to be the most appropriate and efficient method of gaining evidence regarding the complex processes involved. The interviews, with samples of young people and social services personnel, were designed to ascertain their experiences of decision making forums and processes, their understanding of participation, when it is important and how it can be encouraged. With a practice initiative in mind we were particularly interested in identifying conditions that facilitated participation and the scope for improvement.

When adults undertake research with children, extra methodological and ethical issues arise. These issues and how they manifest in the research project can tell us a lot about the actual phenomena under study. Gaining access to children and young people can be particularly problematic (Butler and Williamson, 1994). The extent to which children and young people are enabled to give 'informed consent' will often be dependent on the individual adults who formally have responsibility for the child. Our attempts to negotiate access to and with 'looked after' young people gave us a valuable insight into the organisational setting and the power 'responsible' adults have over children in their care.

Formal permission from key gatekeepers to conduct the research was a relatively simple, if lengthy process. Permission to approach 'looked after' children and young people was obtained from senior social services managers. Following lengthy discussions with managers, it was agreed that whilst 'informed consent' would be sought from the young person themselves, parents would not be approached. To some extent, this decision was made easier by the purposeful choice of a sampling frame of older young people (all 15 and 16 year olds 'looked after' on a particular day).

The dilemmas and potential conflicts surrounding parental and child consent are myriad. There were undoubtedly young people in our sample who would have been mortified if their estranged parent had been approached for permission for the young person to have been interviewed.

On the other hand, the changing balances of power, introduced by The Children Act (which strengthened the rights of parents as well as the rights of children in some areas) would not be upheld by attempts to secure a child's view without the formal consent of parents. Would we or the formal gatekeepers have felt comfortable about excluding parents if the young people were younger, say 9 or 10 years old? What would we have done if the child was keen to volunteer but the parents refused?

The importance of sensitively achieving a balance between the rights and interests of young people and those adults who have responsibility for them was mirrored in our findings. Participation by 'looked after' young people was greatly influenced by the juxtaposition of parental and professional involvement in the decision making process. The young people that we interviewed often found the presence of parents at decision making an inhibiting factor in their ability and desire to express their own views and opinions. The dilemmas facing social researchers as to who, morally and ethically, should be approached for consent over and above the child informant themselves can be seen to be reflected in the decision making processes that pertain to 'looked after' children and young people.

Negotiating access at the more informal levels and with young people themselves created further dilemmas. In our attempts to observe standards that placed the well-being of the research subjects as paramount, we considered that making direct contact with young people (randomly selected from a client record system) could be experienced by young people as an intrusion into their privacy; they may feel intimidated or under pressure to comply, shy or nervous of a stranger or diffident, uninterested. The option of contacting children and young people directly by letter or in person was mediated by initially making telephone contact with their social worker. In this way, children and young people came to hear about the research and our request to interview them through someone they knew and were familiar with. We then followed up our request directly with the young person direct in a manner that was guided by the carer's knowledge of the child him or her self.

This strategy carried considerable risks. We had no knowledge as to the quality or significance of the young person's relationship with their social worker. The strategy placed considerable power in the hands of the social worker to influence the young person's choice of whether or not to participate in the study (by how they presented the research to the young person).

Actually making contact with identified social workers proved to be extremely difficult. A rough estimate would suggest that it took over one hundred 'phone calls to make *initial* contact with fourteen social workers.

Follow up calls to gain feedback from their discussion with the young person were slightly more efficient. Our own experiences of gaining access to young people led us to treat as problematic young people's access to their social workers, the very people most of my informants perceived as the key decision maker in their lives. Finally, some six months into the project we were able to negotiate directly with young people!

There is considerably more literature on the theory and practice of interviewing children and young people for investigative purposes (HO/DOH, 1992; Stainton-Rogers and Worrell, 1993). However, as is noted in chapter 2 of this book, there are still serious gaps in the literature that addresses qualitative approaches to social research with children and young people.

In terms of self-management, the researcher's own experience of working with 'looked after' young people was both a hindrance and a help. This experience made it difficult for us to be 'acceptable incompetents' (Lofland, 1971) and we had to work hard at suspending our own preconceptions and assumptions in order to ensure that we 'heard' what young people were actually saying about their own experiences, rather than what we thought they said. Arguably, adults undertaking research with children will always have to work hard at suspending assumptions. On the basis of their own experience as children, most adults would probably consider themselves 'experts' on children and childhood. As Butler and Williamson conclude:

> the strength of adults' belief in their intuitive understanding
> and knowledge of children has proved remarkable resilient.
>
> (1994:35)

The nature of the research required a flexible and fluid approach to the interviews. A checklist was maintained, which focused on young people's own experiences of participation and their views and opinions on how they should be consulted, on what issues, by whom and in what context. Young people were encouraged to recount their own experiences, both of formal decision making meetings and their wider 'in care' experiences of being involved in or excluded from day to day decisions. The broad areas of interest highlighted in our initial checklist remained pertinent throughout data collection but other topics were added as the research progressed in response to issues and experiences highlighted by young people themselves. In this way, whilst young people had not been involved in the original design of the research we attempted to include those issues which young people themselves considered to be important and relevant to the processes under investigation.

Interviews were conducted at a place chosen by young people, and invariably this was where they were living. At the beginning of each interview, the focus and context of the interview was re-iterated - young people were encouraged to ask questions concerning the research. Many questions were asked - about the research, the proposed outcome and how what they said would be used. The young people we interviewed were very keen that their contribution would be used positively to improve the lot of other young people coming behind them and it was important that whilst we could make no promises about what those with the power to make changes might do with the findings of the study we could at least confirm that we had a mechanism and clear procedure for feeding the findings back into policy development and service planning and a personal commitment to seeing this through. This dialogue proved to be an aide in establishing rapport and assisted in making the event more of a two way process. It also served to support our finding that an important element in encouraging young people to participate in decision making is the young people's belief that they will be 'listened to' and that things will happen as a result.

Ethically, arguably even more than with adult research subjects, it is incumbent on researchers to outline the purposes of research to children and young people and to detail how the information children and young people give to the researcher will be used. Methods of sharing this information will need to vary according to the circumstances and the maturity of the child or young person. In some situations where research links into policy and service development, researchers themselves may have little control over how a particular piece of research is used. However, if possible, young people as research subjects should be enabled to contribute to considerations as to how the research will be employed in policy and service development.

The young people who were interviewed were afforded qualified confidentiality and anonymity. This was explained to young people at the outset of the interview and was not a contract that was entered into lightly. Again, the age and understanding of the young people interviewed in this study eased (but not relieved) the ethical dilemmas that face researchers interviewing children and young people. When conducting qualitative research with children it is important that researchers consider - honestly - the risks to the child subjects that their research involves and how they are going to manage issues that arise relating to harm, risk or neglect of the child or young person.

With justifiable concern as to the potential of researchers to knowingly and unknowingly, exploit children and young people in the course of social research, Alderson (1995) presents a framework for conducting an ethical review of social research projects that involve children. The framework is designed to assist the researcher in assessing the risks and hoped for benefits of the research. Whilst this calculation is complicated, comparing what the researcher considers the benefits might be to countless children in the future (which researchers tend to over estimate), with the risks of harm to the actual child research subjects (which researchers tend to under-estimate) the researcher's first duty must be to the research subjects themselves (Alderson, 1995).

> Risks are hard to predict. Even if a project gains widely-shared approval, a few children may still be upset by it. The harms of coercion, shame or emotional intrusion cannot be measured, though these may be felt so intensely by children that they are unable to express their feelings, and researchers remain unaware of their distress. Researchers need to respond sensitively to children's anxiety, distress or reticence. The main value in discussing risk is to consider which risks might be prevented or reduced, and how to respond to children who do become distressed.
>
> (1995: 2)

In the course of our study no such difficulties were experienced but the important point is that researchers *and their subjects* need to be equally prepared for the risks involved and how disclosures will be managed.

The analysis focused on sifting and sorting key themes from young people's own accounts but it was also relevant to consider our own perceptions of the process that we were engaged in, i.e. adults interviewing young people. When adults undertake research directly on children - the researcher/subject dynamic is superimposed by the adult/child power relationship. Baker (1983) has argued that such reflections can provide adult researchers with valuable insights into ways in which adults and young people interact. Aided by a detailed research diary our reflective approach encouraged us to consider a number of factors relating to the 'interviewing adult's' self management and the young people's ease/difficulty and willingness/reluctance to voice their views and experiences.

Consistently demonstrating a genuine and personalised interest in *what* is said by the respondent (even when it has nothing whatever to do with the researcher's agenda) encouraged rapport, as did displaying some understanding of the processes the young people were asked to recount.

Whilst the size of the study mitigated against arriving at any conclusions regarding the influence of gender, rapport was easier to establish with young people of the same gender as the researcher. Inspiring trust and confidence with children within the limited time frame available to the researcher does pose problems (Butler and Williamson, 1994) but the adult researcher's experience of trying to do so can highlight ways in which children and young people can be helped to contribute to 'adult-based' interaction more generally, including significant decision making processes.

As previously indicated, this research project was firmly linked into policy and service developments aimed at increasing the participation of children and young people in decision making in one local authority. The findings of the study were able to inform policy and practice in a number of ways and to demonstrate that some of the previous responses based on adult assumptions about what would help young people to participate more fully were deficient.

With reference to the research questions this study sought to address, a number of key themes emerge. First and foremost we received a powerful message that young people who are looked after by social services, want to be involved in decision making that affects their lives.

> I want to know all there is to know about my life ... I should
> be there when they talk about me and what's happening. Its
> *my* review after all.

> (Young Person)

They want to be involved at all times, although their interest and ability to participate is likely to increase as they grow older. Being presented with a real choice was important to young people.

A further significant theme arising from the study was that participation has to be viewed as a process not just a principle 'wheeled out' for formal decision making meetings. Young people's experiences before they were looked after by social services and their everyday experiences of decision making whilst being looked after, strongly influence the degree to which they are able or willing to involve themselves in decision making processes. In practical terms, meaningful participation cannot be achieved by just ensuring attendance at formal meetings, consultation has to take place in all aspects of a young person's life.

The importance of being consulted about everyday concerns was put very strongly by one young woman:

> For my own identity it's important. That was a big thing for me when I was younger. People to realise that I was a 'personality'. I wasn't just a statistic. Simple things, it would have been nice for someone to say to me, like other youngsters my age 'what would you like for tea tonight' instead of having set meals every day ... I didn't care about nothing, because no one cared about me, I didn't even care about myself eventually.
>
> (Young Person)

Previous responses from policy makers and practitioners to improve the level of participation by young people have emphasised the importance of young people attending formal decision making meetings. Whilst the resulting changes in practice have positively enabled many more young people to attend such meetings than previously (see Stein and Ellis, 1983 and Buchanan, 1993), in some circumstances young people recounted feeling 'forced' to attend such meetings by their social workers. This had inevitably been counter-productive in many cases to effective participation (rather than attendance at meetings) and had also led to an unhelpful focus on formal meetings at the expense of involvement in day to day decisions.

> They tried to make me go to my review but I wouldn't, they are crap - boring. They ask the same questions all the time, I don't see any thing in them, just people talking.
>
> (Young Person)

Policy makers receiving our research accepted that the paradox of forcing young people to attend formal meetings was unhelpful and incorporated the principle of choice over attendance in the relevant departmental policies, training and guidance.

The study did identify differences amongst young people. Some young people felt particularly alienated from a process that they perceive as defined and controlled by adults.

> I just did what I wanted to do anyway, it didn't really matter what they said.
>
> (Young Person)

This perception was most evident in young people who felt they had had no choice about being looked after by the local authority. Their own sense of powerlessness and unworthiness (within decision making processes that adults favour) has thus, been reinforced. They reject the 'adults' way of doing things' for their own 'vote with their feet' approach, reclaiming some of the power on their own terms. Whilst the authority accepted the challenge that this finding poses, further work needs to be done with young people as to what can be done to engage those who are particularly alienated. Lindsay (1989) poses the, as yet, untested hypothesis that incidents of deviant behaviour or absconding may be minimised if young people are enabled to state their wishes, feelings and concerns in a meaningful way.

A key objective of this study was to identify those factors that facilitate participation and thereby the scope for improvement. Whilst young people generally felt they had adequate information on which to base a decision, our findings suggest that young people and social workers often feel that they have a lack of genuine choices. Participation requires young people to feel they have a genuine choice and access to the people who ultimately make the decision.

The study also confirmed the findings of earlier studies (Stein and Ellis, 1983; Gardner, 1987; Hodgson, 1988; Buchanan *et al*, 1993) which suggested that participation, particularly in the formal decision making process, can be greatly facilitated by the availability of a trusted adult or friend. Young people who are looked after have their closest relationships with their front line carers. Three-quarters of the young people interviewed indicated that it was a key residential social worker or a foster carer who positively enabled them to participate in what was going on.

> Having a meeting with my keyworker worked well. He told
> me who would be there (at the review) and said he would
> help me to say what I wanted to say.
>
> (Young Person)

Positive experiences of decision making for young people centred around quality relationships with significant adults.

In addition to carers, social workers and sometimes other young people who are looked after, our respondents felt they would like to have the option of support from someone independent from the agency. One young person felt it was important for young people to have access to someone from outside the 'system':

> Social workers all stick together. When we have a problem,
> it would be good to have help from someone else, to tell us
> what our rights are and what we can do.
>
> (Young Person)

Buchanan *et al* (1993) suggest that such a service enhances the young person's access to redress and representation, encouraging an ethos of openness. Our findings thus confirmed the importance of developing a service which provided independent advocates for children and young people. Young people's accounts also gave the agency providing this service (The Children's Society) important guidance as to how, when, and where this service was likely to be of most assistance to young people in terms of achieving more effective participation.

The majority of young people interviewed found formal decision making meetings daunting and unhelpful. Young people preferred to contribute in informal settings with adults they know and trust. One young person described her most recent review meeting as follows:

> There was the head of social services; the head of the family centre; my teacher, my sister's doctor, teacher and foster parents and my sister. The only people I knew was my social worker, my sister and Gill my foster parent and that was it, the rest were all strangers. I found it hard saying my personal stuff in front of all these people.
>
> (Young Person)

This young person considered that her attendance at the review had not been worthwhile. In the company of 'strangers', she hadn't been able to talk about something that was bothering her (and was still, at the time of our interview, unresolved). She was left feeling frustrated and disillusioned.

Formal decision making meetings need to take notice of what the young person considers as important as well as the agency's concerns if they are to be meaningful participatory forums that young people can feel an investment in. Whose agenda is up for discussion and negotiation is a key factor. Young people need to feel that the invitation to contribute to the agenda represents a genuine desire on the part of the adults to consider their views. Another young person who at the time of interview, was no longer looked after by the local authority, commented:

> I didn't go to meetings or talk at my meetings or nothing. I said I didn't want to go ... there were all people talking, people I didn't know ... I knew what I said wasn't going to make any difference.
>
> (Young Person)

Venue was also felt to be important, with young people preferring reviews to take place where they live.

There was some evidence to suggest that the additional regulations concerning decision making processes regarding 'looked after' children, introduced by the Children Act, actually worked against enabling young people to be involved in decision making, even though this was a requirement emphasised by the Act. A key factor here, for some children and young people, was the involvement of parents in the decision making processes. Again, previous responses by policy makers and practitioners had not (formally at least) taken into account how the juxtaposition of the rights and interest of children and parents would need to be balanced if effective participation by children and young people was to be achieved.

Within the local authority where our research was undertaken, those responsible for managing the formal decision making processes surrounding 'looked after' children agreed to incorporate such considerations in their procedures, enabling where necessary, separate meetings and consultations involving parents and children to take place. Attempts were also being made to 'de-formalise' (as much as regulations will allow) the significant decision making forums, by for example, inviting fewer people, offering young people the choice over venue and time, and creating opportunities for young people to contribute towards the agenda. It was recognised that far more time and effort needed to be allocated to preparatory work with young people (by those adults who are significant to the young person) prior to a formal meeting in order that young people were given real opportunities to discuss those issues of importance to them.

The study highlighted that in order to facilitate participation by young people who are looked after, training, agency support and the monitoring of social work practice needs to emphasise the responsibility of social workers and carers to *positively* empower young people in much the same way that positive action has sought to address discrimination on the basis of race. The agency's commitment to such a course of action has been demonstrated by their involvement in a new initiative designed to enable and assist young people to be more involved in decision making affecting their lives and their endorsement of this piece of research. The changes, however, required in the mainstream organisational culture of the agency, should not be underestimated.

Perhaps most importantly, our study highlighted the fact that young people have important and relevant things to say about the services they are receiving and the processes that 'responsible' adults are meant to involve them in. It also emphasised how crucial it is that innovations and changes designed to improve the extent of young people's participation are adequately monitored with particular reference to the supposed beneficiaries.

The observations and reflections regarding the methodological and ethical considerations of undertaking qualitative research with children are presented in the hope that they can contribute to the continued development of research which promotes children's accounts as an essential element of service evaluation and development. Undertaking research with children and young people does pose additional difficulties and dilemmas to researchers that need to be debated and reviewed if we are to succeed in making children's accounts more 'visible' and central to policy and service developments.

References

Alderson, P. (1995), *Listening to Children: Children, Ethics and Social Research*, London: Barnardo's.

Archard, D. (1993), *Children - Rights and Childhood*, London: Routledge.

Baker, C.D. (1983), A Second Look at Interviews with Adolescents, *Youth and Adolescence*, Vol. 12, No. 6.

Buchanan, A. (1993), *Answering Back: Report by Young People Being Looked After on the Children Act*, Department of Social Work, University of Southampton.

Butler, I. and Williamson, H. (1994), *Children Speak: Children, Trauma and Social Work*, London. Longman.

Cleveland (1988), *Report of Inquiry into Child Abuse in Cleveland*, Cm. 412, London: H.M.S.O.

Fisher, M. (1986), *In and Out of Care: The Experiences of Children, Parents and Social Workers*, London: Batsford.

Gardner, R. (1987), *Who Says? Choice and Control in Care*, London: National Children's Bureau.

Gillick v West Norfolk and Wisbech Area Health Authority, (1986), AC 112.

Hewer v Bryant (1970), 1 QB 357.

HO/DOH (1992), *Memorandum of Good Practice on Video Recorded Interviews with Child Witnesses for Criminal Proceedings*, London: H.M.S.O.

Hodgson, D. (1988), Participation not Principles, *Insight*, 2/8/1988.

Lindsay, M. (1989), *Perspectives on Child Advocacy*, Unpublished paper presented at Children's Rights in Action Conference, Leceister University, 19/4/89.

Lofland, J. (1971), *Analyzing Social Settings: A Guide to Qualitative Observation and Analysis*, Belmont: Wadsworth.

London Borough of Brent (1985), *A Child in Trust: The Report of the Panel of Inquiry into the Circumstances Surrounding the Death of Jasmine Beckford*, London Borough of Brent.

London Borough of Greenwich (1987), *A Child in Mind: Protection of Children in a Responsible Society. Report of the Commission of Inquiry into the Circumstances surrounding the Death of Kimberley Carlisle*, London Borough of Greenwich.

London Borough of Lambeth (1987), *Whose Child?*, London Borough of Lambeth.

Millham, S., Bullock, R., Hosie, K. and Haak, M. (1986), *Lost in Care: The Family Contacts of Children in Care*, Aldershot: Gower.

Packman, J., Randall, J. and Jacques, N. (1986), *Who Needs Care? Social Work Decisions about Children*, Oxford: Blackwell.

Page, R. and Clark, G. (eds) (1977), *Who Cares? Young People in Care Speak Out*, London: National Children's Bureau.

Rowe, J. (1984), *Long-term Foster Care*, London: Batsford/B.A.A.F.

Shaw, M. (1989), *Social Work and Children's Rights*, Unpublished paper presented at Children's Rights in Action Conference, Leceister University, 19/4/89.

Stainton-Rogers, W. and Worrell, M. (eds) (1993), *Investigative Interviewing with Children*, Milton Keynes: Open University Press.

Stein, M. (1983) Protest in Care, Jordan B. and Parton N. (eds) *The Political Dimension of Social Work*, London: Blackwell.

Stein, M. and Ellis, S. (1983), *Gizza Say? Reviews and Young People in Care*, Bradford: National Association of Young people in Care.

The Children Act, (1989), London: H.M.S.O.

United Nations (1989), *Convention on the Rights of the Child*, New York: UNICEF.

8 Accounting for 'child prostitution'

Anne Crowley and Gera Patel

This chapter considers some implications of a study that examined the involvement of children and young people, under the age of 18, in prostitution (Butler, Shaw, Cowley and Patel, 1994). The study was commissioned and funded by a consortium of social work agencies, representing both the statutory and voluntary sectors, who were concerned to identify the extent and nature of young people's involvement in prostitution and subsequently establish a service response. In this chapter, we will demonstrate the importance of basing service responses on an understanding which relates to the experiences of children and young people themselves, rather than on adult assumptions about the nature of young people's involvement in prostitution and what sort of service is required. With reference to previous research and our own experiences of conducting a small local study, we will examine some of the particular methodological challenges presented to researchers when they attempt to carry out qualitative research with young people 'at risk'.

The idea of 'child prostitution' causes considerable unease. There is a tension between what we associate with the innocence and simplicity of childhood and what we imagine to be the morally depraved world of prostitution.

The transgression of the idealised construction of what adults want to believe is 'childhood', has serious consequences for young people. Benevolence is translated (via the need to 'protect' children) into punishment. Between 1989 and 1993, the numbers of young people under 16 years of age, cautioned for soliciting, doubled (Lee and O'Brien, 1995). As well as being criminalised young people involved in prostitution are pathologised and punishment is re-defined as help. The media often portray stories that shock and sensationalise the issue and seem more interested in asking young people explicit questions about what they do and how much they earn, rather than obtaining accounts from young people as to their reasons for selling sex.

Our understanding of young people and their involvement in prostitution thus provokes different responses from service providers. Traditionally, 'child prostitution' evokes a protectionist response from the welfare agencies, with adults seeking to rescue and protect young people from the 'evil of their ways'. Discussions on child prostitution at Area Child Protection Committees commonly fall under the agenda heading of 'self-harm'. There is pressure to see children off the 'streets' (the symptom) but apparently little attention to why they got there and what could happen to them afterwards (the causes and effects).

Conventional policy and practice responses to 'child prostitution' focus on the child or young person as the 'problem'. In the main the people who are arrested and end up with a criminal record are the young people themselves. It is, however, worth reminding ourselves that if there were no customers to buy the sex from the young people, the young people would not be there selling it. There is a notable gap in the literature on the users of young prostitutes - we do not, it seems, readily accept that adults are regularly abusing and manipulating young people and children into sexual activity.

How we understand the nature of young people's involvement in prostitution is significantly influenced by the views we hold about the value and importance of young people and their own accounts. How we set about gaining our understanding - the methods used and the questions asked - will shape the nature of our understanding and thus the service responses deployed. A study conducted for the Canadian Government, by the Badgeley Committee, recommended that criminalisation would be the only effective way of providing guidance and assistance to juvenile prostitutes. Lowman's (1987) critique of this study effectively demonstrates how the research focus and approach can provide its own answers:

> By focusing almost entirely on the choices made by young prostitutes, rather than on the social milieu in which choices are made, the Badgeley Committee pre-emptively locates the explanation of youth prostitution at an individualistic level. It pathologises the prostitute.

> (1987:100)

Lowman argues that young people's own accounts have been marginalised, leading to deficient, largely ineffective responses.

Qualitative research with children and young people is rare. Indeed, in most social science research, children are absent or invisible (Alderson,

1995). Qualitative research with children and young people 'at risk' poses particular challenges. Making contact with young people who are engaged in both an illegal and stigmatised activity presents obvious difficulties and ethical dilemmas. Many young people have good reason to mistrust the adults in their lives, further limiting the likely success of the adult researcher's approaches. Researchers will need to devote considerable time and effort to the access negotiation stage of the research project if they are to mediate these inherent barriers. Notwithstanding these difficulties, it is important that researchers gain access to as broad and representative sample as is feasible within the research resources available. Ethically, researchers need to consider the likely impact of their research, be it oral histories, in-depth interviews, or observation methods. Research designs which focus important and broad interpretations and understandings on a handful of chance conversations (no matter how revealing) can be damaging to the interests of the 'group' under study.

The risks of causing harm and distress to the research subjects themselves will need to be minimised, where possible, by ensuring the offer of a clear link to an acceptable form of support which will be available long after the researcher has moved on. Prior to undertaking qualitative research in this field, careful consideration must be given to how evidence of harm and risk to young people will be managed.

Agencies working with young people 'at risk' have highlighted the importance of providing a clear framework for the interaction with the young person (Butler *et al*, 1994; Stein, Rees and Frost, 1994). Young people need to know what will happen to the information they impart to the researcher. Circumstances in which confidentiality cannot be maintained will need to be spelt out clearly, enabling young people themselves to make informed choices. If and when a breach of confidentiality is required, young people should be fully informed that this process is happening and an explanation given as to why. Young people should be enabled to take optimum control of the situation.

Given the nature of the phenomena under study and for the reasons outlined above, those undertaking qualitative research with young people involved in prostitution, will need to negotiate the freedom to offer a high threshold of confidentiality - young people can not be expected to talk about their involvement in an illegal and stigmatising activity if they are told that any suspicion of harm to themselves will be reported to the statutory agencies. On the other hand, a framework which allows discretion as to a more imminent and life-threatening degree of harm to the young person, can provoke difficulties for researchers (particularly lone researchers) and it will be important for those undertaking such research to

127

prepare professional and ethical guidance and support that can be pragmatically applied.

The starting point for our own local study centred on attempting to gain a better understanding of the experiences of young people themselves in order that we might assist service planners to provide more meaningful service responses than hitherto. Considerations of what interventions might prove productive demanded a particular focus on the processes whereby young people become involved in selling sex, their lifestyles and the risks they face, and the processes which influence a young person's continuing involvement in prostitution or a withdrawal from such activities.

Our choice of methodology was essentially qualitative, in order that we might gain information about these processes. Data collection centred on young people themselves and those working directly with young people on the streets. Our choice of methodology, combined with the lack of commonly understood definitions, made it difficult for us to discern wholly accurate estimates of incidence and prevalence, even on a local level.

A comprehensive literature review identified key themes and research questions that were particularly pertinent to the basis of service planning and development. These included:

- Definitions of 'child prostitution'

- Explanations of 'child prostitution', i.e. background, development and situational factors, direct and indirect influences

- Lifestyle and risks

- Gender issues

- Past service responses.

In addition to interviews with young people, a number of interviews and consultations were conducted with national and local projects working with young people involved in prostitution. The primary aim of the interviews with young people was to give them the opportunity to raise and explore issues that were important to them, rather than merely relying upon the agencies' and workers' perspective. Young people's involvement in the research study also meant that they would be able to influence any future service development in this area of work. It was crucial that young people were allowed a voice on this issue and for the commissioning group to listen to what young people had to say.

Access to young people was initially negotiated via agency workers in contact with young people involved in prostitution and thereafter by 'word of mouth'. This strategy ensured there was a back-up support network for young people to utilise, if they so desired. Progress towards an adequate and representative sample was hampered by a lack of research time and resources. In addition, one of the statutory agencies involved, was, belatedly, reluctant to sanction access to young people for whom they had a responsibility. Despite these difficulties and limitations, young people did express interest in the research and wanted to contribute to improving services for other young people 'on the streets'.

By far the greater part of the literature on 'child prostitution' focuses on the lifestyles and circumstances of young people engaged in prostitution. This focus has the potential to 'spoil' the actual subjects of any research in this field, as they are defined and studied largely in terms of their prostitution. The potential for a much more rounded account of prostitution is foreshadowed in McMullen's view that:

> prostitution is a behaviour - not a person - and prostitution is
> merely a term which describes a person's behaviour.
>
> (1987:35)

Definitions are important and as Glauser has argued, social scientists' and policy makers' talk about 'street children',

> contains many hidden assumptions about the meaning of the
> family, 'the child', 'the home' and 'the street' which must be
> unpacked and explored to help overcome conceptual
> problems.
>
> (1990:139)

Commonly accepted definitions convey something of the wealth of received ideas and unhelpful moralising that influence any general understanding of what is meant by the term 'prostitution':

> to offer (a person, especially oneself, or a person's talent) for
> unworthy purposes.
>
> Collins English Dictionary

> to degrade by publicity or commonness; openly devoted to
> lewdness; given over to evil.
>
> Chambers English Dictionary

to sell (one's honour etc.) unworthily; put (abilities etc.) to wrong use; debase.

Concise Oxford Dictionary

Issues of definition are particularly important because they reflect and even create the boundaries around understandings of appropriate service responses. Definitions of behaviour effect consequent prevalence and incidence estimates. Generally speaking broader definitions will lead to larger prevalence estimates (Best, 1989). We adopted a broad, readily operationalised definition of prostitution for our own study, namely:

Prostitution involves the exchange of sexual services, sometimes but by no means exclusively, sexual intercourse, for some kind of reward; money, drink, drugs, a meal or a bed for a night.

The boundaries with other behaviour such as paedophilia and pornography remained tentative, but this definition closely approximated to the working definitions assumed by the young people with whom we spoke.

For our purposes, young people were defined as those under the age of 18 years, both male and female. The researchers also decided to concentrate on young people who work on the streets and in clubs and pubs, as opposed to those who operate as 'call' girls/boys or in massage parlours or saunas. There were two primary reasons for this decision. Firstly it is in relation to this type of activity that most information is readily available, but also because it is at this point that prostitution is most accessible, not just for study but for intervention as well. The streets are where most young people begin their 'careers' in prostitution and also where the stigma, risks and dangers are probably at their greatest.

The largest strand of previous research in this field has focused on disentangling aspects of causes and effects. The main independent variables that have been explored are experience of child sexual abuse and, to a lesser extent, running away and homelessness. Some of the best studies have attempted to distinguish direct and indirect casual explanations. McCarthy and Hagan (1992) implemented a sophisticated design which included stealing food, serious theft and prostitution as dependent variables, and unemployment, hunger, shelter problems, coercive parental control, sexual abuse, school experiences, and family intactness as independent variables. Boyer's (1989) thorough qualitative design proved to be an innovative attempt to combine the control of key variables with a recognition of the young person's own understandings and explanations of their behaviour.

We were not aware of any longitudinal studies, and this is part of the reason why we know little about the extent to which young people move in and out of prostitution, or about the likely difference between incidence rates, point estimates of young people involved in prostitution at anyone time, or period prevalence estimates of numbers of young people involved over a period of, say, six or twelve months.

As Lowman (1987) has pointed out, research into young people's involvement in prostitution has all too often marginalised young people's own accounts. Lowman's concern that the choices made by young people involved in prostitution should be viewed within the 'social milieu' in which those choices are made, was echoed by respondents in our study and underpins our subsequent recommendations for service responses. As Marx observed, while people choose to act in certain ways they do not do so in circumstances of their own choosing. For young people the choice to prostitute occurs in the contexts of their marginal position in the labour market and the power of adult males within their families.

Service responses need to be take cognisance of the choices and constraints that young people themselves actually encounter rather than those choices adults think young people freely make. Existing services tend to be based on either a notion of free choice (the 'bad' child prostitute), on no choice at all (the 'vulnerable' child prostitute) or a combination of both. Such explanations provoke paternalistic and protectionist service responses, which ignore the realities of young people's own experiences.

Certainly the young people in our study initially cited some type of monetary gain as a motivation for entering into prostitution. However, it is of crucial importance to note that most young people are unlikely to 'earn' huge sums of money, and any money earned is likely to be spent on essentials rather than luxuries.

> I thought this is disgusting but when I never had no money I
> used to just go to the station cause that was the easiest,
> quickest way of getting money ... well when you used to go
> on the run for days on end, you used to need clothes and
> food and fags.
>
> (Young Person - Male)

There are more complex issues involved. For some young people an entry into prostitution may be for a form of companionship and security. This phenomena was particularly apparent for young people who had been estranged from their parents and families and those that were in or had recently left local authority accommodation.

> I was estranged from my parents and didn't have friends and
> I started going out just picking people up because I thought
> they cared for me, and at first the money didn't come into it,
> it was just spending a night with somebody.

> (Young Person - Male)

Coercion was also cited as another factor in this context, with adults either befriending or targeting vulnerable young people and then pushing them into prostitution and ensuring that they stayed there through physical threats, emotional extortion and dependency.

Workers in the field and researchers are divided as to whether the experience of previous sexual abuse leads directly or indirectly to prostitution. The direct model suggests that sexual abuse leads to a loss of self worth, where abuse degrades and prostitution further degrades. This is succinctly illustrated in Lowman's study by a young person who was involved in prostitution:

> If I was going to stay at home I was going to get screwed, so
> why not leave home and get paid for it?

> (1987:104)

The indirect model proposes that the experience of previous sexual abuse sets in a train of other events such as running away from home, which can lead to a lifestyle based on participating in risky activities, such as prostitution.

The weight of evidence in the literature points to an overwhelming prevalence of disruption and discord in the early lives of children and young people. There is widespread though not universal agreement that sexual abuse, neglect, problems at school, social class, membership of young offender peer groups, unemployment, problems of shelter, and life on the streets are particularly associated with entry into youth prostitution.

Background, development and situational factors, direct and indirect influences are all ingredients in explanations of child prostitution. An important recent American study of youth on the streets demonstrated persuasively that shelter and unemployment are the two most important situational factors explaining prostitution, and that coercive parental control, sexual abuse and delinquency at home are the main background and development factors that directly influence taking to the street, and indirectly influence prostitution (McCarthy and Hagan, 1992). It is also important to note that the events which trigger entry to prostitution may be different for young males and females (Butler *et al*, 1994).

We were able to discover only a few ethnographic accounts of the everyday lives of young people involved in prostitution. But these taken together with the findings from our own small study present a consistent picture of an impoverished and uncertain lifestyle both emotionally and materially, filled with risks to health and physical safety.

Evidence from our local study enabled us to amplify the particular risks for children and young people involved in prostitution, namely risks to health, violence from clients and pimps, and the risks of drug dependency. The last two may ensure that a short spell in prostitution will quickly veer towards a full time 'career'. Local and national agencies agreed that young people were significantly more vulnerable than older people who are selling sex. Young people were thought to be less streetwise, less assertive and less likely to have access to resources aimed at harm reduction.

Our own view is that young people generally possess a high level of awareness of the potential risks to them.

> AIDS was the most (worrying aspect) and getting hurt.
> Them two are definitely ones to worry about.
>
> (Young person - male)

However, they are not always in a position to act upon their awareness. For example, they may not have condoms but feel desperate enough to take risks even though they are aware of the implications, or they may be in a drug or alcohol induced state and not be fully aware of what they are getting involved in. Others may be under the control of a threatening adult.

The literature indicates that as well as the risks of HIV and sexually transmitted diseases, the general health and well being of young people (including emotional well being and mental health) is placed at considerable risk. This is particularly so when prostitution is combined with intravenous drug use or combined with homelessness and living on the streets. Work in the USA (Yates *et al*, 1991) comparing the health of homeless people involved in prostitution and homeless young people not involved, noted significantly higher incidence of infectious disease, including sexually transmitted diseases, pregnancy, uncontrolled asthma and pelvic inflammatory disease amongst homeless young people involved in prostitution.

The potential for getting further involved in or being introduced to some type of drug use presents an added risk. Young people either become involved in prostitution to support their expensive drug habit, and perhaps that of their partner and pimp as well, or use drugs as a form of escapism to forget what it is that they are involved in. Young people may also use drugs as a coping mechanism to give them that extra bit of confidence. The danger here is that drugs that are sporadically used as a coping mechanism can quickly and easily become the primary purpose of being involved in prostitution. It is therefore not surprising that some adults will intentionally introduce young people to more addictive drugs as a means of gaining their dependency and loyalty, and then any money that is earned by young people. Drug addiction may also mean that young people take greater risks, by either sharing equipment or engaging in unprotected sex for more monetary gain.

There is little qualitative work or even administrative or statistical data to indicate the prevalence of physical violence perpetrated against young people involved in prostitution. As with most crimes of sexual exploitation, there is likely to be considerable under-reporting of offences by victims who may fear the initial response and investigation by police and the danger of losing face in a sub-culture where being seen as 'weak' could be dangerous. The young people we interviewed were aware of the risk of violence and took what they saw as harm minimising steps to reduce risks to themselves and others in their peer group.

> When I first started out I used to think 'Oh God I wonder if he's going to kill me' or whatever. Whose going to know because like you heard of lots of prostitutes being killed and stuff ... Most of the time, I would go with my friends to make sure that we were safe ... so there is always someone looking out for you, you know, if it goes wrong ...
>
> (Young Person - Male)

The 'policing' of prostitution can also increase risks, when the only means available to some young people to pay fines imposed, may be to go back on the streets. There is also recurrent anecdotal evidence (Butler *et al*, 1994) to suggest that the specific targeting of a geographical area by the police displaces the activity to another part of town. In such circumstances regular 'safe' clients may be lost and informal support and warning networks are threatened, thus increasing the risks faced by young people.

The criminal aspect of prostitution is one that raises particular concerns when it involves young people. Although prostitution itself is not illegal, the majority of methods of contacting and attracting clients are. The local police that we interviewed explained that the increase in cautioning of young people for soliciting was part of a national trend to 'crack down' on child prostitution. As the law currently stands, an adult cannot be prosecuted for living off immoral earnings unless someone, (e.g. the young person) has been convicted for being a 'common' prostitute. However, it is debatable about how helpful this procedure is to young people. Criminalising young people only increases their marginalisation and furthermore does not get to the root cause of why young people are involved in prostitution. Another aspect of this procedure is that it places little, if any responsibility on the clients of young people. One of the workers we interviewed commented on the hypocrisy that this procedure involves:

> It is just an unbelievable double standard. On the one hand we are shrieking about poor young people getting abused and how we must rescue them, and on the other hand 13 year olds can get a criminal record for being involved in selling sex.

There were also concerns that young men face a greater risk of verbal and physical abuse from the police. It seemed that they were being punished not just for being involved in prostitution but also for possibly being gay as well. One young person recounted that taunts such as 'AIDS spreader', 'pouf' and 'queer' were not uncommon, at the police station. Another young person felt the police were not always sympathetic towards young men whom they knew were involved in prostitution:

> I have had heaps of friends who have been attacked and stuff, my friend was chucked off a car park by a guy and the police just didn't care what he was going through. I have had friends who have been raped and stuff and the police just don't care, they say that male rape is impossible.
>
> (Young Person - Male)

Previous research suggests there are further gender differences between young people who are involved in prostitution. The 'organisation' of prostitution can vary according to the gender of the young person. Women's activities are more commonly reported to be under the control of a 'pimp', and whilst the pimp may also be a source of danger to women, it may be that the anticipation of his existence offers a degree of protection from the use of physical violence by clients. Male prostitution is less commonly pimped, it would seem, and operates somewhat further away from the street lights; for example in parks and public toilets (Bloor *et al*,

1990).

The nature of the power relationship between young men and their clients sometimes exposes them to a significant degree of risk. Bloor's (1990) ethnographic study of rent boys in Glasgow, for example, indicates that a significant proportion were engaging in unsafe sex and were not always getting paid for what they did. This was evident in our study, where young women said they had picked up 'tips' from older, more experienced women who were working on the streets. Consequently young women were apparently more likely to charge the 'going' rate and get their money up front. Young men were more likely to engage in unsafe sex, charge considerably less, and sometimes not be paid at all. One of the agency worker's we interviewed made the following observation:

> The working practices of the boys and the young women, the differences are huge. You would never get a woman going with a punter for £3 and no condom. They (young women) negotiate terms before they get into the car, they get paid before they do it. Now the boys, £3 a go and no condom, that's totally unacceptable to the girls.

Service responses

Service responses are unlikely to eradicate prostitution amongst young people and attention needs to focus on how service providers can work with young people themselves to minimise risks of harm. The risks of harm facing young people involved in prostitution are considerable. Our findings indicated that young people themselves have an awareness of the risks involved and ways in which these risks can be minimised (including peer support) but they do not necessarily have the support systems and organisational structures that can assist in reducing the level of risk.

Services operating within a harm reduction framework are more commonly provided to adults selling sex. For perhaps obvious reasons, such a way of working can be seen as more acceptable with adults than with children and young people. Notwithstanding the difficulties facing agencies who attempt to grapple with the inherent moral and ethical dilemmas, in the course of our study we were able to identify a small but impressive range of more innovative street based services that targeted young people. These services all operate within a harm reduction framework, working on the streets undertaking outreach work. Workers supported young people with advice, information and counselling as well as practical resources such as condoms. Workers were also involved in advocating on behalf of young people to obtain services from statutory agencies.

We have previously drawn attention to the traditional service response which when faced with what is seen as isolated cases of 'child prostitution' seeks to rescue children and young people, sometimes forcibly removing them from the streets and placing them in secure accommodation for their 'own safety'. Our local study, supported by the experiences of national agencies working throughout the United Kingdom (e.g. Green, 1992) indicates that policy makers and service providers need urgently to accept that 'child prostitution' is not an isolated phenomena that can be addressed by incarcerating one or two children or young people. It is only when we accept and 'own' the problem that we can begin to address the reasons why young people are becoming involved in prostitution and help reduce the risks they face. Young people's own accounts need to inform our understanding of the issues involved and the subsequent service responses.

Our own study, indicated that planning for service options in this area of work will need to recognise that services will not always be easily greeted by the intended beneficiaries. Planning will also need to recognise that the young people involved are likely to be distrustful of statutory agencies and to feel the need to talk confidentially to someone who will not judge them for what they have done.

> I think I would have tried to have looked for a support worker or a counsellor, where I could go and talk to someone who wouldn't judge me or make me feel that I was a different person because of what I had done, or try to lecture me. Somebody who would just listen to me, somebody I could have just gone and spoken to.
>
> (Young Person - Female)

This quotation illustrates the importance of giving young people the freedom to explore their options in a safe environment and then allowing them to make informed decisions. Young people may need to talk about their experiences of being involved in prostitution, but may not necessarily feel that they are in a position where they are able to extricate themselves, because of the influence of controlling adults or other dependencies such as drug misuse.

It is of crucial importance for young people to feel that they have retained some sense of control over their lives, but if they divulge information events may occur over which they feel they have little or no control, such as the automatic involvement of social services departments and the police. The fear of such occurrences may prevent young people (as they did with the young woman quoted above) from seeking essential health and other support services. Where Child Protection Procedures are not perceived by young people as 'protecting', the risks involved in disclosure can be seen as far outweighing the risks of continuing to be involved in prostitution.

Service responses must assist planners in developing services which will address the reasons why young people become involved (and remain involved) in prostitution, and reduce the risks of harm that they face. Young people's own accounts encouraged us to promote the importance of developing services that young people will make use of, services they can identify as helpful and supportive. To this end we recommend the establishment of outreach projects specifically focusing on the needs of young people under 18, which incorporate commitments to confidentiality and shelter and to methods of working which emphasise the development of peer support and education and harm reduction. We believe that such services should be provided by voluntary agencies (who will be seen by young people as 'safer' than the statutory agencies), as part of a wider multi-agency strategy.

Moreover, we believe that an integrated service response will take fuller account of the 'whole person'. Our own study corroborated the work of others (McMullen, 1987; Green, 1992) in identifying that young people involved in prostitution have a range of needs in such areas as family relationships, self-esteem, sexuality and the provision of adequate shelter and food. The accounts presented to us by young people made us very aware that responding to one or all of these needs was unlikely to alter a young person's overall situation significantly.

> A lot of people look at prostitution as a dirty thing and I don't think it is a dirty thing. You may be doing it because you feel that you need someone to give you a cuddle, you feel that you need someone to love you.
>
> (Young Person - Female)

Service responses therefore need to take account of the causal and sustaining circumstances of a young person's involvement in prostitution, thus dealing with the issues that lead young people onto the streets to sell sex and not just regarding young people as 'the problem'. Support services available to young people need to be strengthened alongside improvements in housing, benefits, and employment opportunities for young people. In any event, our interviews with young people made it clear to us that young people would be unlikely to make use of a narrowly focused 'prostitution' service, especially one bearing such a label.

A major focus for our local study was to try to gain an understanding of the reasons for 'child prostitution', factors that trigger entry, and the risks involved. The conclusions that social workers and agency managers draw regarding, for example, the relation between child prostitution and the experience of sexual abuse or homelessness will have direct consequences for the kind of services - if any - that are set up. If it is concluded that the issue is one of 'survival behaviour' rather than 'sexual behaviour', it may follow that practice responses that focus either on the prevention or the amelioration of shelter problems among the seriously at risk population, should be promoted. On the other hand, if we are persuaded that sexual abuse leads to a loss of self worth, which in turn leads directly to vulnerability and victimisation, we are likely to be sympathetic with Foster when she advocates that:

> empowerment models of social work are appropriate for young people whose experiences have left them with a sense of powerlessness and dependence upon abusive lifestyles.
>
> (1991:400)

Our experiences of undertaking qualitative research with young people demonstrated the breadth and depth of understanding that can be gained from talking with young people themselves. We have attempted to illustrate how this understanding can be used to inform and develop more effective service responses for young people 'at risk'. It is important that our understanding of the phenomena and the basis of service responses relates directly to the experiences of children and young people themselves and those working on the streets. Experience dictates that we need to focus on why young people are selling sex, what has lead them to the point of selling sex to adults, and how to reduce the risks they face, rather than just simply how to stop them selling sex. If we do not deal with the actual issues *from the perspective of the young people involved* and effect the appropriate changes in society to prevent young men and women selling sex, nothing will alter.

Our study confirmed that for young people involved in prostitution, 'child prostitution' is less about morality and more about homelessness, poverty, a lack of love, and of belonging. It is about child sexual abuse and the exploitation of children and young people by adults. Put another way it is about the *failure* of adults to promote and safeguard the welfare of children and young people. Perhaps that's the 'account' we don't want to hear and why instead we continue to punish the children. As Freeman suggests, the syndrome of blaming the child victim is firmly entrenched in our culture and is perpetuated by the status of children and young people in our society:

> Public issues like bad schools and youth unemployment, all too often become the private troubles of children, truancy and delinquency. The private ill suffered by children who are abused is part of the public problem of a culture which cannot accept children as persons entitled to dignity and respect

(1987:300)

In the final analysis, 'child prostitution' cannot be regarded as an isolated phenomenon which is freely chosen in a social vacuum, but as part of how we view the exploitation of power through age, gender, race and class throughout society.

References

Alderson, P. (1995), *Listening to Children: Children, Ethics and Social Research*, Barnardo's, London.

Bloor, M., McKeganey, N. and Barnard, M. (1990), 'An Ethnographic Study of HIV Related Risk Practice Among Glasgow Rent Boys and their Clients', *AIDS Care*, 2, pp17-24.

Boyer, D. (1989), 'Male Prostitution and Homosexual Identity', *Journal of Homosexuality*, 17, 151-184.

Butler, I., Shaw, I., Crowley, A. and Patel, G. (1994), *Paying the Price?* School of Social and Administrative Studies, University of Wales Cardiff.

Foster, C. (1991), *Male Youth Prostitution,* University of East Anglia.

Freeman, M. D. A. (1987), 'Taking Children's Rights Seriously', *Children and Society*, 4, 299-319.

Glauser, B. (1990), 'Street Children: Deconstructing a Concept', in James, A. and Prout, A., *Constructing and Reconstructing Childhood*, Basingstoke: Falmer Press.

Green, J. (1992), *It's No Game: Responding to the Needs of Young Women at Risk or Involved In Prostitution*, Leicester, National Youth Agency.

Lee, M. and O'Brien, R. (1995), *The Game's Up*, London, The Children's Society.

Lowman, J. (1987), 'Taking Young Prostitutes Seriously', *Canadian Review of Sociology and Anthropology,* 24, 99-116.

McCarthy, B. and Hagan, J. (1992), 'Mean Streets: The Theoretical Significance of Situational Delinquency Among Homeless Youths', *American Journal of Sociology,* 98, 597-627.

McMullen, R. (1987), 'Youth Prostitution: A Balance of Power', *Journal of Adolescence,* 10, 35-43.

Stein, M. and Rees, G. (1994), *Running the Risk,* London, The Children's Society.

Yates, G. L., Mackensie, R. G. and Swafford A. (1991), 'A Risk profile Comparison of Homeless Youth Involved in Prostitution and Homeless Youth Not Involved', *Journal of Adolescent Health,* 12, 545-549.

9 How do young Asian and white people view their problems? A step towards child-focused research

Ilan Katz

Children's lives are regulated and planned by adults. Most adults who plan services for young people would claim to be acting in the best interests of children, and they believe that they understand what children need. Children themselves are rarely represented either directly or indirectly. Adult agendas define the concerns which society deems to be important about children (Stainton-Rogers and Stainton-Rogers, 1992), and these concerns are constructed by particular historical forces and events (Gergen *et al*, 1990). The human sciences have been dominated by this adult focus in which young people are seen as objects of study rather than subjects with their own valid constructions of the world (Caputo, 1995).

Children have very strong ideas about what they want and need (Butler and Williamson, 1994) and there is evidence that they are able to accurately identify the quality of services offered to them (Hill, 1995). Children from black and minority ethnic communities are doubly marginalised within mainstream sociology and psychology, and accounts of their needs and expectations are virtually absent from the literature (Gilroy, 1987; Stanfield, 1994; Stopes-Roe and Cochrane, 1990).

This chapter describes a research project which attempted to address some of these issues. The research method consisted of focus groups with young people. It formed part of a needs assessment project relating to services for children with emotional and behavioural difficulties, which also included a questionnaire survey and interviews with health, social services and education professionals. The research was commissioned by a health authority in a deprived area of northern England with a high resident population of young people of South Asian heritage.

The aims of the research were to:

- elicit the views of vulnerable young people about the nature of the problems facing them,

- discover the way they dealt with those problems,

- find out what were the sources of support which they could call upon and

- ascertain their feelings about the health and welfare services.

The material gained from these focus groups, and from the interviews with youth workers, teachers and other Asian professionals, was to be used by the health authority to plan services for young people with emotional and behavioural difficulties. A particular focus of the research was an attempt to gain the views of young men and women of South Asian heritage, who were seen as under-represented within the client profile of the agencies, but whose needs were believed to be at least as great as those of the white child population.

Six focus groups were held with young people at youth centres in various parts of the area. Altogether 57 young people attended these focus groups, ranging in age from 13 to 20 years. Numbers at individual groups ranged from 5 to 11, with the average number being seven. The young people who attended these groups were not selected because they were users of health services - they were simply those people who were present on the day of the focus groups and volunteered to discuss the issues. Nevertheless it turned out that several of the focus group members had experience of one or the other of the services. The young people were paid a small sum of money to cover expenses. Because of the nature of the youth clubs the groups were organised as follows:

- two mixed groups of white young people aged 14 to 17,

- two groups of Asian young men aged 15 to 20 (one of which was attended by three white young women),

- one group of Asian young women aged 14 to 15,

- one group of young Asian women aged 17 to 18.

Youth centres rather than schools were chosen as appropriate venues because the youth and community service caters for vulnerable young people, ie potential users of services for children with emotional or behavioural difficulties, in non-stigmatising venues.

Shaw has referred to the potential applications of focus groups in Chapter Two. In this study focus groups were used because they are groups consisting of members who interact already, and therefore provide a relatively safe environment for young people to discuss their perceptions. They allow in depth exploration of the issues without any assumptions being made about the likely range of responses, and in consequence enable different perspectives to emerge. Focus groups mitigate the power imbalances between the young people on the one hand and the researcher and commissioners of the other (Morgan and Kreuger, 1993). The focus groups were structured so that the young people could discuss their perceptions of their own problems and individual needs. In accordance with accepted focus group methodology this format was adopted because it could not be assumed that young people would view the issues in the same way as professionals or researchers (Zeller, 1993).

The core questions for the focus groups included:

1. What do you think are the main problems facing young people like yourselves?

2. If you had (or have had) an emotional problem, who would you turn to for help?

3. How would your family deal with emotional or behavioural problems?

4. Do you see any differences in the problems of Asians and white young people, and between young men and young women?

5. What services do you think should be available to help young people with problems?

6. If you were in charge, how would you spend the money on services for young people?

Although each group covered these areas, they all spent most of the available time discussing the issues which they themselves chose as the most significant. For example both groups of Asian young men focused on racism, their families and their relationships with their own cultures. The white young people discussed family problems and school difficulties.

In all the focus groups the researcher was accompanied by a youth worker who normally worked with the group. This was an invaluable aid in keeping the group focused on the inquiry topics, and also created a link with the 'normal' youth work. In some cases the youth worker decided that issues which were raised in the focus group would be further discussed in later sessions. In the groups of Asian young people the youth workers were essential because they enabled the session to be conducted in a culturally sensitive manner.

Problems faced by young people

All the focus groups opened with the question 'What are the main problems facing young people like yourselves in Northshire?' There was some consensus within the groups about these problems. However, the different groups expressed different priorities in relation to them. The table below is a broad summary of the main issues raised.

Table 9.1
Problems identified

	White	Asian
Young Men	boredom, lack of facilities, school, relationship with parents	racism, relationships with parents, arranged marriages, jobs
Young Women	school, relationship with parents, relationships with young men, pregnancy	arranged marriages, racism, sexism, relationship with parents

What is noticeable about the response of the young people is that their conception of need was, in general, very different from that of professionals. Most professionals expressed need in terms of a lack of services for children and young people. The young people themselves, however, need much more in terms of either broader categories such as unemployment or much narrower categories such as particular family problems and difficulty in school. Only occasionally did they relate these to a lack of mental health or welfare services.

There were some shared problems and some differences between young men and young women, white and Asian young people and also between older and younger individuals.

Shared concerns

Perhaps the best example of consensus was that most young people said that one of their problems was 'boredom'. For example, a young Asian said,

> ... yes we come to the youth club some days, but it is not always open for us. Other days we just hang around, we've got no money to go into arcades or the cinema, so there is nothing much to do ... we don't like going to each other's houses because we want to be away from the parents.

A young white man in a rural area said,

> I go to Benham as often as possible because it's more fun there and sometimes we go to Northchester. I wish there was something nearby for us to do.

Many of the young people claimed that boredom led them into such activities as drug use, under-age sex, petty crime and 'gang fights'. Another problem shared amongst most of the young people was complaints about school, especially that they were being pushed too hard at school, that the teachers were unsympathetic and unhelpful and that school was boring. The third area of shared concern was difficulties with parents.

Differences between the sexes

Despite the above similarities, the majority of problems faced by these young people differed between the groups. In some ways the group that stood out from the others were the Asian young women who tended to lead very different lives from their brothers and white young people. For example, all the white young people, as well as the Asian young men, had encountered or been involved with under age sexual activity and drug use. Many had had dealings with the police. The Asian young women, however, tended to have much less contact with any of these issues. Only a few of them, for example, had had any contact with drug taking. This difference was confirmed by the youth workers, who said that Asian women tend to be kept very much in their own homes, and were less likely to attend the youth centres for recreational purposes. One young woman said:

> We're very different from the white girls in school. We come home, help our mothers with the housework and watch television. We aren't allowed out to clubs or places like that ...

> Our parents don't even like us coming to the youth centre ... if I go off the rails in any way they will just make me get married.

Many of the Asian young women contrasted their situation to that of their brothers and also their classmates. They felt that women are badly treated by the Asian community. For example they are expected to achieve academically as well as helping out at home, whereas their brothers are not expected to contribute to the household chores. There is more pressure on them to get married at an early age. Although both Asian young men and women said that they were forbidden to have boyfriends and girlfriends, some have done so. It was clear that the pressure on young women not to engage in premarital sexual activities was much greater than the pressure on men. Their families gave them very little opportunity to see young men on their own. Asian young men themselves acknowledged that life was more difficult for their sisters than it was for them.

The young Asian women also contrasted their own situation with that of their school friends. White girls of their age are allowed to go out, have boyfriends and do the things that western teenagers are expected to do. Young Asian women said that they lead much more restricted lives than white young women and are generally not allowed out of the house. Some young Asian women felt jealous that their lives were so restricted compared to that of their school friends, but these opinions were not universal. Some felt that they were better off than white teenagers because they were much less likely to become pregnant, or abuse drugs. A female youth worker in one of the groups said:

> I think that the community looks after women very well.

It was interesting that young Asian women seemed to see no alternative other than their own restricted lives or the possibility of single parenthood, drug abuse and prostitution. Some of them also felt that the pressures were less on them than those on young Asian men. Young men have to deal with broader society and pressures on them in the workplace were hard. They also had responsibility for looking after the family, and in some respects, therefore, their lives were more difficult than for young women. In general there was a strong feeling that young Asian women were isolated and felt restricted and vulnerable within their community.

There were few comments from white young women about their treatment as women, although they were clear that their needs differed from those of the young men.

Family relationships and pregnancy

Although almost all the young people said that problems with parents were of major concern, these problems differed considerably from group to group and between individuals within groups. A common complaint was that parents were too restrictive and did not allow them to do what they wanted. However, it was apparent that there were major differences between white and Asian young people in this respect. For example young Asian men seemed to live a completely separate life from their parents. In one of the groups young men described how they go out, and take soft drugs, drink alcohol, engage in sexual activity (mainly with young white women) and sometimes engage in criminal activities such as car theft or driving under-age. They believe their parents have no idea about these activities. They very seldom discuss issues with their parents and have developed sophisticated ways of preventing parents knowing about whereabouts.

One young man said:

> My parents only got to know about what I was doing when the police called at their door after I was caught driving my brother's car. This was when I was fourteen years old. My father didn't believe what I'd been up to but when he realised it was true he really beat me up.

The use of physical punishment was a common theme among Asian young men and women. Many described situations where they had been beaten by parents, older siblings or other relatives for various misdemeanours. Very few of the young Asian people felt supported by their parents or able to discuss emotional or relationship problems with them.

In contrast the responses of white young people were very mixed. Some of them felt that their parents didn't care at all about them, whereas others felt quite close to one or other parent and able to discuss quite intimate issues with them. A young white man who was interviewed with his mother said:

> I always go and talk to you, Mum, don't I? Whenever something bothers me at school or outside I discuss it with Mum and she helps me. My brother is completely different though, he never discusses anything with anyone.

Several white young people described how their parents spent a lot of time drinking and did not really care where they were or what they were doing. No white young person mentioned physical chastisement.

Several of the young white women mentioned the possibility of becoming pregnant as an issue for them. However, they did not see this as a major problem and were quite fatalistic about the possibility. Many of the professionals, however, expressed great concern about the numbers of young pregnant women who were unable to cope with babies. Some young women seemed to feel that the possibility of pregnancy was just one of the dangers they faced. Perhaps this was because they had not actually experienced pregnancy themselves. One of the young women in the focus groups was in fact pregnant but she did not perceive it as stressful and seemed to be rather proud of her situation. This issue seems to be confined very largely to the white population. Asian young women expressed fear and horror about the possibility of becoming pregnant. The consequences for them would be exclusion from their own community and family.

Racism

Both groups of young Asian men, and one of the groups of young women felt that racism was the main problem which they faced. They experienced it at school, in the workplace and the streets. One young man said:

> We haven't got any money so we have to hang out on the streets. Also we are not allowed into pubs because if a member of our community spots us in a pub they will tell our parents. The problem is that when we are out on the street white boys come up and try to beat us up. Now, we are getting back at them as well and there is a war going on between us.

Another young man told this story:

> I was walking down the street and a young kid - he was about four years old - said; 'black bastard'. His dad came out and said to him; 'No you don't call him a black bastard, you

go out, get a baseball bat, hit him on the head and then call him a black bastard'. That really scared me.

Another young man described how he had repeatedly telephoned a local company and asked for a job application form to be told that it was a waste because there were no jobs. When a white friend had contacted the same company minutes later he was immediately sent a form, even though the company knew nothing about either applicant's experience or background.

Some of the young Asian men said that they no longer were prepared to be victims, and that they now defend themselves or even actively seek out whites to attack. Others felt that violence was not the best way to respond to racism. Several young men described racist incidents by both pupils and teachers in school situations, but this was not universal and some schools were praised for the absence of racism. Interestingly both white and Asian participants accused their teachers of favouring the other group.

> I don't know why it is but they always put us Asians together in a group. There are only three other Asians in my class and we always get put into the same group with each other, even though we don't like each other. Also, we get blamed if there is any trouble.
>
> Young Asian woman

> The teachers always blame white children. Whenever there is trouble, no matter who starts it, the whites are always given the blame and then we get a lecture about racism.
>
> Young white man

Another interesting finding was that some young Asian women seemed to feel little effected by racism. Although some of them described incidents where they had been called names in the street and at school, they said that this was just teasing and did not see it as a major issue which affected them or their feeling of wellbeing. Their perception was that racism was confined largely to schools. This view contrasted with that of the youth workers and other Asian professionals, who tended to feel that young Asian women were, if anything, more affected by racism than young Asian men as it exacerbates the sexual oppression to which they were subjected. Some professionals cited a research study to show that black women were doubly disadvantaged in the job market. In discussion some of the youth workers felt the young women were being protected from racism by the community and that the effects on them were indirect rather than direct. They would confront racism directly only if they entered the job market or had a lot of contact outside the community.

Young white people took a different view. As mentioned above they felt that teachers supported Asian pupils. Some white group members held racist views themselves. One young man said:

> I think they should all go back to their own country ... send them back, that's what I say.

He claimed that one of his friends had been beaten up by a gang of young Asian men.

Young Asian people felt there was little work being done directly within schools to address the issue of racism and their perception that teachers were, if anything, more racist than their classmates was particularly worrying. Teachers felt that racism was a problem that was imported into school from outside and there was little that they could do to combat it. It is clear from these discussions, and also from the interviews with youth workers and teachers, that there is a great deal of racial tension in the area and certainly young Asian men feel racism is a major factor.

The focus groups did not establish that racism in itself effected the emotional wellbeing and self-esteem of young Asian men. In the groups young Asian men did not appear to have lower self-esteem or to be emotionally more damaged than their white counterparts, despite the fact that they were under considerable pressure from racism. One worrying feature of the discussions was the lack of support for young Asians who suffer racism. Very few said that their parents would support them. On the contrary, parents advised them to ignore or avoid it. Teachers and other adults were also seen as unsympathetic, and most young people said that they would not talk to anyone.

From the young white peoples' point of view, racism was just one of several 'tribal' antagonisms; young people in two local towns expressed distaste for each other, and young people from different areas within the towns formed groups which were very antagonistic. It does seem, however, that racial divisions were more significant than these other territorial conflicts. There was very little evidence of any real friendships across the racial divide and Asian and white young people felt they inhabited very different worlds.

Arranged marriages

Young Asian people placed arranged marriages high on their list of problems. Obviously young white people did not mention arranged marriage at all and none even referred to long-term relationships. Both young Asian men and women complained that they were being coerced into marriages, often without discussion and against their will. Many said that their siblings or friends had been tricked into marriages and several told stories of young people who were told they were going to Pakistan on a holiday only to be whisked off to a wedding ceremony when they arrived. Some of the young people felt that they would have some choice and that they could refuse partners who were not acceptable. The majority, however, felt that they would be unable to refuse, and they would have to accept their parents' first choice. Some young people felt that marriage was used by their community as a way of preventing young people from deviating from the 'norm'. Young women in particular felt they were expected to get married while they were still teenagers and that their parents only let them study further because they felt they would be able to claim a better marriage partner. There were also several descriptions of young people who had run away from home rather than be married to the partner of their parents' choice.

Although they started out expressing universal antagonism towards arranged marriage, when questioned further some of the young women felt that, in principle, arranged marriage was not a bad idea. They did not believe that the western concept of marrying for love was a guarantee of a successful marriage. What they objected to was being married to relatives in Pakistan who had a completely different upbringing, and where attitudes towards women were more oppressive than those of local Asian young men. One young woman of Bangladeshi origin said that this was not the pattern in her community, and young Bangladeshi women are not expected to marry their cousins. All the young women felt that, however the marriage was arranged, it was very important for the husband to be a Moslem and for their religion to be perpetuated.

Generally speaking young people felt that the institution of arranged marriage was acceptable but they wished to have more control over the selection of the marriage partner and the timing of the marriage. It was clear that arranged marriages were a major source of stress for both young men and women in the Asian community and they felt that there was very little they could do about it and few people with whom they could discuss the problem.

Employment

There were contrasting views between professionals and young people about employment. Professionals described how lack of employment affected families and communities. Chronic lack of opportunity in the area meant that many young people had no prospect of regular employment or even wanted it and were living their lives expecting to be helped out by the state. Unemployed parents spent much of the day drinking and this affected their relationship with their children.

Within the focus groups, however, only the young Asian men saw employment as a major problem. There was heavy social pressure within the Asian community for men to have some sort of employment, and many of the young Asian men felt that many of their difficulties with their parents would be solved if they had a job. Some of their fathers were unemployed, which had adversely affected both their self-esteem and family life. The young Asian women felt that marriage was more important than employment and even those who planned to have a career saw marriage as being the primary focus of their lives. Surprisingly, young white people did not feel that employment was very significant. Some of them had part-time jobs and these seemed to be relatively easy to obtain. The youth worker who attended one of the focus groups felt that because of their age, these young people had not yet entered the job market and were therefore still 'blasé' about their prospects for employment.

Drugs and alcohol

Youth workers and teachers mentioned the use of drugs and alcohol as being an increasing problem especially in the urban areas of Northshire. The under sixteens in this sample did not generally admit to using heavy drugs but youth workers mentioned eight and nine year olds who regularly got drunk. This is often related to their parents' drinking habits. Professionals tended to feel that these problems were less prevalent in the Asian community, but the focus groups indicated that for some young Asian people at least, drugs and alcohol were as much part of their lives as for young white people. Young people themselves did not see the use of drugs or alcohol as particularly problematic. Drugs were in regular use as part of their recreational activities and young people felt that they would continue to use drugs in this way rather than to abuse them. Alcohol was slightly different for young Asian people. They felt ambivalent about its use because alcohol is forbidden in the Moslem religion and this caused a lot of guilt amongst young Asian men.

For example one young man said:

> We are all involved in drinking but we have to be careful that our parents don't find out or we would get into deep, deep trouble. I know that it is wrong and I suppose that when I become a parent I'll stop my children from drinking.

Youth workers felt drinking and drug-taking in the under sixteens were a symptom of lack of opportunity and poverty rather than being difficulties in themselves.

Sexual relationships

Several of the young people described sexual relationships as a major problem. Again, this affected white and Asian young people differently. For young white people, the difficulty was expressed as the expectations of boys and girls regarding how sexual activity should occur and feeling rejected by members of the opposite sex. None of the young people acknowledge being homosexual.

Asian young people faced the additional problem of having to keep their relationships secret. Young Asian men said that they very seldom have relationships with young Asian women, and most of them saw young white women. They had to avoid walking on the streets with their girlfriends because they might be seen by a member of their community and their parents would find it unacceptable for them to be involved with a white person. Both young Asian men and women said that if it was discovered that they were involved in a committed relationship they would be compelled to get married very quickly. For this reason they felt unable to discuss with their parents the emotional problems of their peer relationships and this placed them under even more strain.

Religion and identity

Asian young people talked a great deal about religion. Most of them had a rather ambivalent relationship towards Islam. On the one hand most were quite detached from the practices of religion saying that they attended mosque less often than they should or than their parents, and often they transgressed Islamic laws. Some expressed bitterness about the treatment they had received at religious schools where physical methods of discipline were apparently often used. On the other hand all felt very strong commitment to the religion. Many mentioned that they would become more religious again when they themselves become parents. Religion also offers them some comfort and guidance and some of the Asian youth workers said that they often get queries from young people about whether particular activities are within the Islamic law or not. Keeping the religion alive was a priority for all the young people.

By contrast, religion was not mentioned at all by any of the young white people. The impression was that they had very little contact with religious institutions or authorities.

In several of the groups the topic of identity was raised. Most of the young people identified themselves as 'Asian'. Most had been born in this country, and identified themselves as British, (but not English). Virtually all have been to their country of origin, and all said that they had enjoyed their time there. Several of the young people expressed a desire to live in Pakistan or Bangladesh, but others felt much more comfortable in the UK. Their main identification was with Islam. Identity was complex and seemed to depend on the context of the discussion rather than being a fixed entity (See Stopes-Roe and Cochrane, 1990 and Scantlebury, 1995 on this point)

Emotional support

The young people were all asked, 'Who do (would) you talk to if you had an emotional or relationship problem?' The table below summarises their responses.

Table 9.2
Who would you talk to?

	White	Asian
Young Men	no one, friends	no one, brothers, uncles
Young Women	friends, mothers, fathers, youth workers	no one, friends, mothers, youth workers

Like the previous question this tended to be answered differently between the sexes and the races. In general girls were much more willing to discuss problems with their parents, especially their mothers. White girls in particular tended to name their parents and their friends as *confidantes*. Asian and white men said that they would not discuss problems with anyone at all. When pushed, however, many of the Asian young men said that they would talk to older siblings or other relatives. White young men initially insisted they would talk to on-one but some said that perhaps they might talk to their friends.

Virtually all the young people said that they would not discuss problems with any professional. None of them said they or their families would go to their GP or to a social worker. Those who had been involved with a social worker were slightly more positively disposed towards them but even they felt that social workers had not been very helpful. One young Asian woman described an incident which illustrated the inappropriateness of some services for her community:

> When I was about twelve I was having a lot of problems at home, and I spoke to the teacher about it. The next thing I knew a social worker had been around to my house and put a note through the door, because there wasn't anyone at home. No one asked me about whether I would like them to come or anything ...
>
> When my mum found out she told my brother and they beat me up badly. The next day the social workers came back. I told them that the problem had gone away, and they disappeared. I had to do that because they threatened to tell my dad, and he really would have beaten me up.

This story illustrates the difficulty for young people who do take the plunge and confide in professionals.

Some said that they would speak to individual, trusted, youth workers. One group of young Asian men felt that there should be counsellors based in schools who are young and Asian and who have had similar experiences to the pupils. Young white people also favoured a similar idea. Some, however, were suspicious of any counsellor or adult who might help them. Some felt that going to a professional, especially a social worker, would suggest that they were considered mad or inadequate by the community.

Parents

When asked, 'What would your parents do if they found that you had an emotional or relationship problem?', the young white people generally felt that their parents would be upset and would try to talk to them about it. Some of them said that they would be prepared to talk to their parents but others said that they would avoid their parents. Some said that their parents might discuss the problem with their teacher or someone else at school. The young Asian people gave a different response. Most said that their parents initially would respond by hitting them. If that did not work then their parents would either take them to an Imam (a religious teacher) who would offer some advice or they would send them back to Pakistan, probably to have them married. Alternatively the parents might feel that the child has been cursed and take them to somebody who would exorcise the curse. There was a strong feeling amongst the Asian young people that their parents did not acknowledge emotional difficulties and saw them either as disciplinary issues or as a magical curse.

This picture confirmed the views of many practitioners who felt that Asian families were much less likely to refer to professionals than white families and much less likely to acknowledge the emotional basis of children's problems. One the major pressures that young people felt was that their parents, even if they were sympathetic to them, felt the need to emulate those who set community norms and statuses ('keeping up with the Joneses') and therefore felt compelled to keep their children under control. Young people felt, therefore, that even though their community was closely knit this was based on keeping up appearances rather than on real concern for each other. Some of the young people also complained that gossip and rumour were rife within the community and this could affect the way parents felt able to help their children. For example parents needed to ensure that their children seemed to be 'normal' and this encouraged them to deny the children's problems. A further complication is that children who had been involved with professionals might have their marriage chances adversely affected and might even prejudice the opportunities of their siblings. This was another factor which encouraged parents to deny children's emotional problems.

Despite these views, some responses were at variance with those of professionals. For example several of the young people felt that going to the Imam had been a useful experience and he had offered very good advice. Others felt that the Imam was only 'in it for money' and that their parents had sometimes spent hundreds of pounds for such superficial advice as 'Don't hang around with those boys at the canal'.

Many felt that going to Pakistan and meeting their extended family had been very beneficial to them when they had emotional problems.

> I got on much better with my uncle in Pakistan than I ever got on with my own family. They treated me like a prince and I was allowed to do all sorts of things. I could talk to my uncle about things that I could never talk to my father about.
>
> Young Asian man

Many of the young Asian people, especially men, had run away from home for short periods. Professionals said that young Asian men and women running away from home was one of the major challenges facing the services. For young Asian people, running away from home involved higher stakes than for white young people because they were likely to be ostracised from the family and the community. Some described friends and acquaintances who had been completely "cut off" despite living very near to their own family. It seems that despite the enormous implications some young people felt that the only way that they could express their emotional problems was by running away. There seemed to be few places for them to turn to when there were severe family difficulties and very little to prevent young people from leaving before a crisis occurred.

Discussion

The views expressed by members of the focus groups indicated that young people in Northshire were faced with a range of financial, relationship and emotional problems with few resources to enable them to confront these issues. They felt unsupported by their families, schools or the professional establishment and they relied mainly on themselves or their friends for advice and support.

It is also apparent that the situation of white and Asian young people, and of young men and young women is perceived to vary considerably. Although all young people face some common problems they were dealt with differently from one community to another, and also within communities. Each community has its own strengths and weaknesses, and it is not possible to say that a particular group was 'worse off'. Although there were some variations between different Asian communities, the young Asian people stressed the similarities rather than the differences.

How are we to interpret evidence gained through these focus groups? This research highlighted the question of the interpretation of sensitive information provided in the course of the field work. The responses of the young people interviewed may have been biased by the fact that they were talking to a white male researcher whom they had never met, notwithstanding the fact that the young people denied the researcher's race had affected the discussion. The youth workers expressed surprise that the young people had been so forthright about themselves and had focused on one discussion for over two hours.

A difficult problem was the interpretation of the views of young people when they conflicted with those of the professionals and of currently accepted accounts of the reality of young people's lives. Examples mentioned above included racism, employment, drug use, and pregnancy. All these were areas where adults identified problems, but where at least some of the young people saw no problem. Adult researchers and professionals may have good grounds for believing that young people are suffering from various degrees of 'false consciousness' ie that they are in some way deluded as to the true nature of the problems confronting them. However, it is impossible to be sure where and how this applies.

The basic dilemma is, either the researcher accepts at face value what young people say about their lives with the consequent risk of failing to discover and address underlying issues which are not expressed, or s/he feels able to interpret young people's responses, with the danger that the research will then become adult-centric.

This dilemma is particularly difficult for anti-racist or feminist research paradigms based on notions of empowerment. These paradigms have the ostensible *raison d'etre* of giving a voice to marginalised groups of people whose voices have been suppressed by mainstream social science (Lather, 1992). The problem is that empowerment models maintain that re-interpretation of the material is an unwarranted use of the researcher's privilege over the subjects. The researcher has no right to claim that s/he has any privileged position from which to interpret the participant's viewpoint (Guba and Lincoln, 1989). On the other hand, simply repeating what young people have said, although tempting, is both naive and disingenuous, for two reasons.

First, retelling the views of young people without comment is not *practically* possible. The attempt not to mediate the voice of the subject ignores the processes of selection of the material which the researcher must inevitably enter into. This selection in itself will inevitably affect the way it is perceived by the reader. More importantly, the gender and race of the researcher, the way the original questions were framed and the context of the field work may have affected the original responses. Thus any notion that the researcher's role is to act as a mouthpiece for marginalised voices without mediating between the participants and the reader, must be misguided and naive.

Second. repeating the views of young people without comment is *theoretically* naive. Social constructivist paradigms seem to be empowering; they allow marginalised subjects to portray their own constructions of the world, and offer different perspectives from those of mainstream social science or professional knowledge. However, as Stanfield (1994) points out, these paradigms assume that disempowered and marginalised individuals have the same latitude to construct their own beliefs and identities as middle class white people. He argues that powerful social forces are operating on these constructions, limiting the available constructions of marginalised people. Unless this is taken into account, the research will inevitably become part of the Euro-centric discourse of social science.

159

The implications of this analysis are that an Asian young woman may well claim that her major problems are to do with parental restrictions on her freedom and deny that racism plays any part in her life. Although these may be very 'real' feelings, honestly expressed, they may, at least in part, reflect the powerful images of 'normal' adolescence which surround the young woman in the media, at school and in personal relations with white peers.

This is not to imply that the views of these young people are any less valid than those of professionals or indeed the researcher. The latter are similarly mediated by social constructions. However, the discussion should point to some of the difficulties for a sociology which attempts to adopt an explicitly empowering stance towards children and members of other marginalised groups. The research described here should therefore be seen as representing a first step on a long path towards addressing sociology's neglect of the voice of children and young people from minority communities.

References

Butler, I. and Williamson, H. (1994), *Children Speak: Children, Trauma and Social Work* London: Longman.

Caputo, V. (1995), Anthropology's Silent 'Others': A Consideration of some Conceptual and Methodological Issues for the study of Youth and Children's Culture in Amit-Talai, V. and Wulff, H. eds *Youth Cultures: A Cross-Cultural Perspective* London: Routledge.

Gergen, K. J., Gloger-Tippelt, G. and Berkowitz, P. (1990), The Cultural Construction of the Developing Child. in Semin, G. R. and Gergen, K. J. (eds) *Everyday Understanding: Social and Scientific Implications* London: Sage.

Gilroy, P. (1987), *There Ain't no Black in the Union Jack*, London: Routledge.

Guba, E. G. and Lincoln, Y. S. (1989), *Fourth Generation Evaluation*, Newbury Park: Sage.

Hill, M. (1995), The Views of Young People about Care and Social Work Services *Child Care in Practice* Vol. 2, No.1.

Morgan, D. L. and Kreuger, R. A. (1993), When to Use Focus Groups and Why in Morgan, D. L. (ed) *Successful Focus Groups* Newbury Park: Sage.

Lather, P. (1992), Postmodernism and the Human Sciences in Kvale, S. (ed) *Psychology and Postmodernism*, London: Sage.

Scantlebury, E. (1995), Muslims in Manchester: the depiction of a religious community *New Community* Vol. 21, No. 3.

Stainton-Rogers, R. and Stainton-Rogers, W. (1992), *Stories of Childhood: Shifting Agendas of Child Concern,* Hemel Hempstead: Harvester Wheatsheaf.

Stanfield, J. H. (1994), Ethnic Modelling in Qualitative Research in Denzin, N. K. and Lincoln Y. S. (eds) *Handbook of Qualitative Research* Newbury Park: Sage.

Stopes-Roe, M. and Cochrane, R. (1990), *Citizens of This Country The Asian-British,* Clevedon: Multilingual Matters.

Zeller, R. A. (1993), Focus Groups on Sensitive Topics: Setting the Agenda without Setting the Agenda in Morgan, D. L. (ed.) *Successful Focus Groups* Newbury Park: Sage.

10 So much for 'participation':
Youth work and young people

Howard Williamson

The sociology of youth has, by and large, been preoccupied with the deviant, the spectacular and the bizarre. The main bodies of study fall broadly into two camps. One has focused on 'ritualised resistance' through youth cultural styles, from the Teddy Boys in the 1950s to punk rock and rave culture in the 1980s and 1990s. The other has explored the ways in which young people make transitions to the labour market, an area of study given financial momentum by the dramatic increase in youth unemployment in the late 1980s.

There have, of course, been more specific, but related foci of sociological inquiry on themes such as gender (eg Griffin, 1985; Scanlon, 1990) and race (Cashmore and Troyna, 1982). All, however, have two features in common. First, they testify almost exclusively to the real, inherent powerlessness of young people in controlling decisions about their own lives. Secondly, with few exceptions (Jenkins, 1983; Davis, 1990; Blackman, 1995), they fail to give much theoretical or empirical consideration to more ordinary young people, nor to those receding areas of social policy in which the interests of young people are explicitly centre-stage rather than subordinate to wider economic and social imperatives. Indeed the prevailing contemporary view is that social policy relating to young people has moved inexorably away from the days in which the post-war social democratic consensus sought to construct an approach based on 'winning consent', to a climate in which 'coercing compliance' has become the order of the day (Davies, 1986; Williamson, 1993). Therefore, at the levels of both empirical inquiry and theoretical analysis, it is argued that children and young people are pawns in a wider political and professional game, able only to effect 'magical' and imaginary, rather than real, solutions to the predicaments they experience (Cohen, 1972; Mizen, 1995). They are oppressed, disempowered and excluded from any platform on which the real decisions affecting their lives are made.

Nevertheless, there is an arena of social and educational policy which continues to claim that practice is formulated through a genuine process of dialogue and consultation: the youth service. The practice of 'informal education' of young people during their leisure time rests, albeit on an increasingly precarious base, on a principle of *negotiation* and at least rhetorical assertions that youth work with young people should be premised upon objectives such as 'participation' and 'empowerment' (Smith, 1988, 1994; Jeffs and Smith, 1990b). At the very centre of the development of youth service provision lies the goal of 'meeting the needs of young people', although these needs have always been mediated by a variety of organisational objectives and social priorities. Such organisational and social imperatives may have assumed greater weight in recent years, but youth work has historically been guided (implicitly at least) by Carl Rogers famous maxim: 'I cannot teach anybody anything, I can only provide environments in which they can learn' (Rogers, 1983). In youth work, such environments can only be constructed in relation to the subjectively expressed needs and motivation of participating young people. This is so because participation is *voluntary*. Inappropriate and unattractive provision is likely to cause young people to 'vote with their feet'. The voluntaristic nature of involvement by young people in youth work, coupled with the youth service's remit to reach out to those young people who are most disadvantaged and marginal to other institutional provision, might suggest a need for the repeated endorsement of the centrality of young people's decision-making in the shaping of youth work practice. Recent developments, however, suggest otherwise, indicating that one of the remaining spaces in which there has always been a clear professional responsibility to hear the voices of young people above competing demands may be being steadily eroded.

In the pursuance of research evidence on the effectiveness of youth work (and, critically, that its 'person-centred' philosophies are being sustained even in the face of external pressures), the case for qualitative methods seems unequivocal. The problems of inquiry hinge, predictably, on the usual research problematics of reliability and validity. Such issues have surfaced dramatically in recent years on account of the political and managerial requirements placed on the youth service to measure progress and outcomes and to evaluate performance. This pressure has led to a renewed emphasis on often superficial 'number-crunching' (in essence, who took part in what), which pays scant regard to the *quality* of interaction and experience available in sites of youth work practice - a matter which is clearly more contentious and less 'reliable', yet ultimately potentially a much more plausible measure of youth work impact and performance, in terms of both its philosophical base and its practice rationale. Monitoring records of programme delivery, participation and attendance may well be a reliable measure of provision and usage, but they tell us virtually nothing about the *educative* experience, levels of active participation, or contribution to 'empowerment' (or, indeed, their absence!). Only the use of qualitative methods - through participation, observation and listening to the voices of youth workers and young people themselves, thus permitting analysis based on the 'triangulation' of data sources (Hammersley and Atkinson 1995) - can *illuminate* the efficacy of youth work interventions and the nature of the youth work experience. It was the adoption of such an approach which informed research inquiry into the development of the youth work 'curriculum' in Wales and which exposed divergent understandings, attitudes and assumptions about the purpose and impact of youth work provision and practice, particularly in relation to the changing political and professional expectations placed on youth work delivery in recent years.

The changing context of the youth service

The paradox in the contemporary context of youth work is that there *has* been confirmation that youth service provision should be 'person-centred' while simultaneously there has been a drive to connect that provision more firmly to wider priorities in youth policy such as health promotion, crime prevention and vocational preparation.

The main impetus for these developments has been the three Ministerial Conferences on the Youth Service, which took place between 1989 and 1992. These conferences were a substitute for the inquiries into the role of the youth service which had been conducted at approximately ten-year intervals over the previous three decades. The first of these previous inquiries, the Albermarle Report (Ministry of Education 1960), confirmed the need for 'social educational' provision for young people and recommended the construction of purpose-built youth centres and the rapid establishment of a professional service. The second, the Milson-Fairbairn report (Department of Education and Science 1969), emphasised the community context in work with young people and promoted the concept of a 'youth and community service'. The third, the Thompson Report in England (Department of Education and Science 1982), paralleled by HMI Survey 13 in Wales (Welsh Office 1984), confirmed - and even applauded - the eclectic methodology which youth workers invoked in order to respond appositely to the needs and aspirations of the young people with whom they worked. This included the provision of *activities, advice and information,* space for *association,* opportunities for *action* in the community and *access* to life and vocational skills. And, just as youth cultural studies had drawn attention to the fact that spectacular youth cultures emerged within young people's leisure time (the 'weak link in the chain of socialisation' compared to family, school and work), the youth service was confirmed as an important (constructive but perhaps also controlling) intervention in that same leisure sphere, providing a participative and empowering space in which young people could *learn* and thereby be better prepared for the rights and responsibilities of adult life.

By the end of the 1980s, however, there was a new, tighter political agenda. Old links in the chain of socialisation had apparently broken down and were failing to deliver. New moral panics were digging in about the 'social condition' of young people, and new expectations were consequently imposed upon the youth service. The youth service was already encumbered with addressing new needs facing young people (eg. unemployment, homelessness), and with dealing with agendas set primarily by its professional workforce (eg. racism, sexism and oppression). Inevitably, alongside its professional partners in the social welfare and educational world, such as social work, probation and teaching, it became subjected to close political scrutiny.

At the first Ministerial Conference, in December 1989, the Minister expressed his requirement that the youth service define its purpose far more precisely. He stressed that a 'concentrated fusillade' was invariably better than a 'scatter gun approach' and wanted to know whether the youth service offers 'value added' or 'deficit model' provision, enhancing personal development or compensating for a lack of personal development elsewhere in young people's lives. He wanted to know about priorities: age groups, target groups, issues, and methods of work. And he wanted to know on what basis progress could be measured and performance could be judged. The Minister called for the establishment of a 'curriculum' for the youth service, though he was at pains to emphasise that this did not have to reflect or relate to the National Curriculum being developed for more formal education (see National Youth Bureau 1990).

The response from the field was initially unhelpful. The 'broad church' of organisations comprising the youth service (ranging from local authority education and leisure departments and voluntary agencies working with young people to uniformed youth organisations) were hard pressed to agree on anything, beyond rhetorical re-assertions that youth work was about personal development and social education for *all* young people (ranging in age from 11 to 25) who wished to take part in it. The service felt under threat, yet offered very little in the way of any coherent counter-arguments (though see Williamson, 1990; Jeffs and Smith, 1990a). Instead, consultations with the field, undertaken by the National Youth Bureau (now the National Youth Agency) in England, gradually established more focus and produced a Statement of Purpose, mapping priority age groups, target groups, issues and methods, and identifying a range of performance indicators. This represented a curriculum for the youth service. At a local level in England, the national (English) statement of purpose has provided the foundation for 'curriculum development'. In Wales, a 'Curriculum Statement for Wales' which draws on and develops the English material has been adopted. In all cases, it is these curriculum statements - emphasising the educative, participative and empowering (and, in Wales, expressive) purpose of youth work, underpinned by equal opportunities - which have come to determine eligibility for the diminishing resources available for youth work provision. They have become reinforced by expectations around the production of business plans, performance targets and outcome indicators, something that has put shivers down the spines of many practitioners in the field. Moreover, at the third and final Ministerial Conference, the Minister spoke firmly of the need for youth work to connect closely with wider social agendas. He cited the role youth work might play in youth crime prevention (something subsequently supported by a Coopers and Lybrand (1994) report on preventative strategies for young people at risk, but dismissed by the Home Secretary as displaying insufficient 'hard' evidence), but implicit in his message was the need for youth work to demonstrate how it dovetailed with new social policy priorities, such as health education and health promotion, and getting young people into training. Such expectations fall well outside the boundaries of conventionally-understood professional youth work objectives, which are about working closely with young people in order to support them in making informed choices (even if, ultimately, they make apparently 'stupid' ones). And they lie even further away from the reasons proffered by young people themselves for making use of youth work provision, which are often, crudely, as a place to meet and an opportunity to engage in the activities available.

Or at least that is what is *assumed*. There is a relative dearth of informed empirical research on the youth service. In contrast, there is no shortage of sometimes rhetorical and often polemical texts on how youth work should be done, ranging from general ideas about experiential learning and informal or 'local' education (Dewey, 1963; Jeffs and Smith, 1990c; Smith, 1994) to ideas more specifically located around youth work (Brew, 1946; Jeffs and Smith, 1987; Smith, 1988; Bunt, 1990). There are historical narratives and analyses about the youth service (Jeffs, 1979; Springall, 1977). There have been texts concerned with the relation between young people, youth work and the wider policy context (Jeffs and Smith, 1988; Willis *et al.*, 1988). Endless surveys of young people have addressed young people's involvement with the youth service to a greater or lesser extent (eg Eggleston, 1976; Brown, 1994), and there have been numerous case study accounts of specific youth work projects (Holden, 1972; Smith *et al.*, 1972; Williamson and Weatherspoon, 1985). But very little work has been conducted which places the qualitative experiences of participating young people at the centre of the research endeavour - something of an irony in view of the still prevalent rhetoric that the youth service is *uniquely* about placing young people centre-stage. The irony persists despite the fact that academic and policy studies in other 'youth policy' areas have paid far more attention to the perspectives of young people as expressed directly by them, see for example, Hirst (1994) on health, Istance *et al.* (1994) on youth training, Dewdney *et al.* (1995) on housing and homelessness, Graef (1992) on young offenders. Throughout the three Ministerial Conferences on the youth service, the voices of only four young people were heard; 'consultations' were almost exclusively limited to senior personnel in the maintained and voluntary youth work sectors!

It is these apparent disparities between the high level 'curriculum' debate and the grounded realities deriving from 'folk knowledge' about youth work practice and young people's experience that generate a fundamental research question: to what extent is the emergent curriculum framework meaningful and relevant to both young people who participate in the youth service and to those who work with them? In turn, the findings arising out of an empirical study of this issue raise a number of critical, more theoretical, questions about the extent to which the rhetoric of participation and empowerment can be sustained in the face of an ever increasing managerial direction in youth work practice.

The research project

There is enormous variation in youth work provision and practice. There are part-time one-night-a-week clubs run by volunteers and full-time centres operating with paid and trained staff. There are 'drop-in' centres dealing with unemployed and delinquent young people and structured programmes of activities organised by uniformed youth organisations.

The sampling approach to the selection of sites of provision has been reported elsewhere (Williamson *et al,*. 1993). Briefly, while not claiming representativeness, it aimed to provide a balance in terms of social, cultural, economic, geographic and demographic factors particular to Wales and to reflect the diversity of provision in the youth service in Wales. Twenty-eight settings were eventually studied. The relevance of this research question is far from being parochial. While there may be *elements* of youth work which bear a specific relation to the Welsh context, it should be emphasised that many cornerstones of youth work practice in Wales are not dissimilar from those which apply throughout the United Kingdom.

The objectives of the research study were to identify the thinking behind and implementation of current practice, to establish some kind of classificatory scheme outlining what counted as 'good' practice and to inform the process of developing a core curriculum for the youth service in Wales.

Fundamentally, workers were encouraged to 'make their case' for what they did, whether or not this lay within any kind of curriculum framework. The research gathered and analysed any written statements informing the work of each setting. Common questions were asked of workers and young people in attendance in each setting and this was complemented by more open-ended discussion. The atmosphere, activities and relationships in which explicit provision was embedded were also observed and recorded. This methodological process of 'triangulation' (see Hammersley and Atkinson, 1995) permitted a construction of a sense of the 'youth work dynamic' which was taking place, within the financial, staffing and spatial constraints bearing on a particular setting. What was, in the first instance, most important was the level of *congruence* between the accounts and perceptions of workers (and between full-time and part-time staff) and those of young people. For, in our view, only a *shared* sense of what was going on could provide a platform for effective development.

This chapter, however, gives priority to the views expressed by young people. Attempting to elicit considered perspectives from young people is rarely easy. There are two fundamental methodological problematics to be overcome. The first concerns the banter, 'piss-taking', flippancy and repartee which invariably precedes more serious reflection on reasons for participation and any ensuing 'educative' experience. The second is that there are usually infinite possibilities for diversion and distraction, if only in the form of friends arriving or an activity starting, let alone an 'incident' which no-one wants to miss. Holding young people's attention - while simultaneously seeking to pursue a serious research agenda - is always a delicate task. Moreover, as a stranger to the setting, there is no guarantee that the necessary trust and credibility will be effectively established. Factors such as image and presentation, or style of speech, may attract the curiosity of some young people but, equally, they may deter or alienate others. Furthermore, young people (particularly those in the most disadvantaged circumstances) may be reluctant to be 'questioned' about *anything* and dubious of the capacity of a 'university researcher' to connect at all with their predicaments. The gathering of data from young people is therefore apparently fraught with difficulty. Yet, paradoxically, young people are often remarkably open and frank in talking to adults who seemingly display real interest and attention to their views. Indeed, strangers/researchers can be a useful receptacle for young people's perspectives and experiences: they are not local, they have no obvious power over them and they are therefore 'non-threatening' in the sense of being able to use divulged information against them at a later date. It *is* therefore quite possible to secure detailed and in-depth accounts from young people (from both individuals and groups), though there will be considerable attrition along the way - as young people 'drop out', lose interest or are sidetracked by more interesting diversions.

The critical research question hinges on the validity and representativeness of those accounts. But that is no different from the accounts of any other 'actors' within the context under study. The actions and attitudes of young people are meaningful and have meaning to them and it is important that research endeavours to grasp those *meanings* and seek to locate them within both the broader context of those young people's lives and the specific context of youth work interventions and experiences which are taking place.

Only by taking proper account of the perspectives of young people - whether or not they are objectively 'accurate' or somehow 'superior' to those held by other stakeholders in youth service provision - can appropriate responses by made and relevant 'services' be delivered. This is not, of course, to argue for simply taking young people's views at face value, responding to them and stopping there. It is to argue that the only effective development and evolution of youth work provision must *build upon* the prima facie case made by young people about the reasons for their participation.

Findings

Why participate? Irrespective of the 'constituency' of young people being served by particular youth work provision, there was a remarkable level of consistency in the responses of young people concerning their views about the purpose of youth work. There was an overwhelming contention that it was a place 'to meet friends and have fun'. The second core reason for attending was to engage in the activities provided. This generally meant the 'usual' youth work menu of table tennis and pool, although most settings had at least one or two more interesting additional activities on offer, such as batik, weight training, photography or dance. For the majority of the young people interviewed, the planned occasional day or residential trip was a key attraction of the club - an integral bonus, rather than an optional extra. Only one or two, however, made explicit reference to participation in those events as a means of offering opportunities for self-realisation, discovery and personal development.

The same applied to sporting activities and inter-club competitions (which have often been vilified at higher levels in the service). Although young people did not expressly mention their value in providing 'involvement and challenge', there was pervasive enthusiasm for such provision because of the fun, enjoyment and social contact they got out of it.

The role of the youth worker These rather 'mundane' but important representations of the *meaning* of youth work are critical points to bear in mind, given the often elevated nature of the youth work curriculum debate. Youth workers are clearly not paid just to unlock the doors to social space for young people. Many are, indeed, keen to extend the parameters of their practice beyond the conventional activities and competitions to the provision of information, advice and support and other more 'educative' interventions, but it is always important to be reminded of the fact that young people's attendance is rarely premised upon such possibilities. Young people do not participate in order to be 'informally' educated.

Virtually no young people in the study perceived the youth work setting as a source of support or advice, nor the youth worker as a receptive 'listening ear', professionally charged with responding to the needs and issues in their lives. Indeed, in many cases, the very opposite was true. Young people viewed youth work provision as an opportunity for *escapism* - somewhere to get away from the 'hassles', anxieties and pressures of the real (and adult-controlled) world, epitomised by home, school or work (or no work). Although some respondents talked of having established trust and confidence in *some* of 'their' workers (never all of them) and of having confided in them, many said they would turn elsewhere, especially to friends or relatives, should they need to talk through means of resolving personal concerns.

Similarly, the preoccupation within the youth service curriculum debate with 'issue-based' practice made few connections with either grounded practice or participants' aspirations. When asked whether or not any 'group work' on issues such as health or sexuality took place, most young people referred immediately to the light-hearted quizzes that occasionally took place. These were often more about pop music, contemporary events or soap operas than 'serious' contemporary issues affecting young people. Although one or two more imaginative workers had exploited the quiz format to address more serious issues, very little other issue-based work appeared to be going on. Nor did young people appear to want it. When cameo examples of what this might entail were conveyed to young people, the commonplace response was that it sounded 'too much like school' and was not something that would appeal to them.

What is clearly implied by this data is that the 'educative' process of youth work needs to proceed in a softly-softly and sensitive way, if young people are not to vote with their feet and stay away. Young people were adamant that too much structure and formality would almost certainly put them off coming. Despite this - and this is a salutary lesson for those committed to establishing a more rigorous framework for the delivery of youth work - many young people claimed that they had in fact 'learned a lot' from involvement in 'their' clubs, displaying a sense of pride and ownership in a range of experiences in which they had had the opportunity to participate.

Participation and Empowerment In over a quarter of settings, young people testified to a high level of participation and consultation - a key component of various curriculum statements on the youth service. Neither the apparent formality of the 'programme' nor the range of resources available (in terms of building size, activities and staffing) were a guide to the presence or absence of real involvement by young people. What seemed to be much more important was an invisible sense of 'culture' or atmosphere, one in which young people were relaxed in each other's company and in their relationships with workers, and confident about expressing their opinions and preferences without fear of ridicule, dismissal or being ignored. Some settings which exhibited this intangible context of creative and positive social interaction had often not moved far beyond it in terms of developing a repertoire of provision, sometimes by 'choice' but more often because of insufficient financial, spatial and staffing resources. Others, however, had established an impressive range of 'interventions', covering a broad spectrum of youth work practice, from routine activities or involvement in competitions, to arts and video projects and engagement with the local community. These had invariably been proposed and stimulated by young people themselves, using workers as advisers, resource consultants and facilitators, in a way not dissimilar from much 'enterprise education' in schools (see Jamieson *et al.,* 1988) and the European youth initiative projects (see De Wachter and Kristensen, 1995).

In contrast, it was clear that not even the rhetoric of participation, let alone the concept, had yet permeated some settings. When asked about involvement in planning and decision-making, young people in a number of settings expressed complete surprise. They viewed themselves as passive consumers of provision planned, organised and delivered by the workers. This view held true in the majority of settings irrespective of their size, and may well have something to say about either the training of workers, the perceived or real expectations of management, or both.

Only in a very modest sense did young people even allude to notions of empowerment. They certainly did not use the word! The most frequently cited 'learning' which they claimed had taken place was that they had become 'more responsible' and more 'self-disciplined', but this is not necessarily evidence of 'empowerment'. For example, there was a realisation on the part of young people in some settings that non-conformity to agreed behaviour resulted in instant banning, sometimes for a considerable period. Less drastic sanctions were also applied to young people who displayed dissent or refused to co-operate in planned events.

In the fewer settings where relationships were more comfortable and confident, there was evidence of 'empowerment', though even there young people were unable to articulate it. Nevertheless, they talked of having become more self-assured through the acquisition of knowledge and skills - practical, personal and social - during their involvement. Critically, they valued the fact that workers tended not to attempt to exercise power over them and that issues were resolved through discussion and negotiation. They were also correct in their confident assertion that workers did not have any real power over them, since their only real sanction was exclusion, which could be pre-empted by self-exclusion - voting with their feet - and these young people were quite aware that workers needed the numbers in, and exploited *that* power accordingly! It is a perception that can equalise the balance of power in youth work settings, and have both constructive and destructive repercussions.

Expression The youth work Curriculum Statement for Wales, unlike its English counterpart, specifically includes an *expressive* dimension as a central guiding force in youth work. It is, reassuringly, around this theme that young people had most to say about the 'learning outcomes' arising from youth work involvement. Young people claimed to have become more competent in socialising, in their general relationships both with other young people and with workers. Beyond the environs of the youth work setting, they maintained that they had become more assertive and confident in communicating their views (sometimes to their cost, since others may be less receptive to the questioning of their authority and their decisions). The vast majority of young people, irrespective of the type of club they attended, claimed to have learned to express themselves more positively or at least to have developed more self-control so that they were less likely to engage in spontaneous aggression.

Young people's views and experiences of youth work - an overview

Youth service provision remains a broad church, catering for a diverse age range (perhaps 7 to 25), delivering a diverse programme, exploiting a range of methods, and claiming to address a spectrum of issues. No wonder there have been attempts to clarify its purpose. But that clarification has been conducted with very little consideration given to the perspectives of young people - a major design fault in a service which prides itself on being person-centred and empowering.

The research reported here was an attempt to restore some balance in understanding what the youth service is about, from the perspective of young people, in order to explore how such views fitted with the perspectives of what the youth service should be about, from the perspective of senior professionals and politicians. The findings are discomforting, though my conclusions will suggest that there is potential for reconciliation.

First, what young people communicated in the research is a far from sophisticated analysis of youth work. Young people choose to take part in its provision for the fun and enjoyment it offers, through the internal and external activities it provides. Few young people admitted to experiencing any significant problems in their lives (though this point might be 'objectively' contested, see Williamson 1993), beyond the general observation that there was 'nothing to do round here'. Younger respondents were at times vaguely aware of local problems, such as the level of unemployment, but this remained a relatively distant 'issue'. There were, of course, older respondents who were acutely aware of the lack of jobs, the prevalence of drug misuse, and the scarcity of independent housing for young people. However, in what might be called 'run-of-the-mill' youth work provision, only rarely did young people say that they would confide it, or seek advice from, youth workers in order to address these issues. There were exceptions to this. Individual workers were identified by club members as people 'you can talk to about everything'. But, more often, young people turned elsewhere for advice and support.

Young people were therefore generally dismissive of issue-based interventions *except* when discussion of issues was triggered by something that had happened to, or been experienced by, them. Learning from issues that directly affected them often proved popular; this is consistent with other accounts of the process of experiential learning (Brandes and Ginnis, 1986; Dennison and Kirk, 1990). The challenge for youth workers is clearly to seize on the casual observation, a specific incident, or a story line in a soap opera, in order to dispense information and advice, and raise awareness, in moments when young people are likely to be receptive.

A second key theme addressed in the research was the 'constituency' of young people served by youth service provision. Although the curriculum debate addressed priority age groups and concluded that the 16+ age group required particular attention, most of the settings surveyed catered primarily for those within the compulsory school age range. Clearly no setting can cater for all young people in a locality, but an important question concerns how actively or passively the 'constituency' served has been determined. The 'targeting' of young people - by virtue of age, gender or other criteria - is certainly problematic but, equally, requires careful attention if more disadvantaged (and older) young people are not to be neglected and effective provision is to be developed for them.

Finally, the third important finding was that many participants in contemporary youth work provision were completely unfamiliar with a philosophy of autonomy and self-determination. The mirror-image view expressed by workers was that, when they had endeavoured to promote greater participation, this had been met by an apathetic response and a lack of reliability on the part of young people. This is hardly surprising, however, given the powerlessness experienced by the majority of young people in wider contexts. It signals a need for caution in expecting too much too soon from youth work interventions while simultaneously reinforcing the need for workers to renew their efforts to ensure that all provision is constructed around the aspirations, needs and involvement of young people. For this to take place, workers need *time*, something which is in short supply when workers are expected to produce relatively short-term evidence of the outcomes of their work.

Youth work provision caters for some very different 'constituencies' of young people and therefore cannot be judged according to uniform criteria. The research suggested that the most effective practice derived from a high level of *congruence* between full-time workers, sessional staff and young people about the rationale and purpose of the work. That practice did not, however, always square with curriculum principles of empowerment and participation, let alone other priorities around age groups, target groups and priority issues. Nevertheless, such congruence reflected shared and mutual understanding, and frequent communication and conversation (see Smith, 1994) between those involved, striking a common path between the aspirations of young people and the responsibilities of youth workers. This 'good practice' spanned a continuum from the 'deficit model' to the 'value added' typologies of provision alluded to at the first Ministerial conference. Some was premised on the strengths of the invisible relationships at play, while other provision was based more around quite overt leadership and motivation, reflecting both the 'enabling' and 'advocacy' models of community development (Cunningham and Kotler, 1983). In contrast, many settings displayed little evidence of congruence, with major gulfs in understanding between the parties concerned. Even many of those conveying a level of congruence were apparently tradition-bound in doing little more than making activity-based provision.

Conclusion

There are two core conclusions to this chapter, one methodological, the other substantive and policy-oriented. The former feeds the latter. With regard to method, there is a central need to find ways of hearing the voices and views of young people if we are to construct an effective framework of understanding within which relevant policy can be shaped. This, in itself, is not a particularly new argument and, indeed, may be applied to policy intervention beyond the youth service, in areas such as youth training and unemployment (Williamson, 1995).

There are, of course, questions about the validity of young people's accounts. The pragmatic response, however, is that while young people's accounts may not have any greater objective accuracy than the perspectives of other stakeholders in the youth service (politicians, managers, educational theorists, and face-to-face workers), it is those subjective views that determine the level of involvement and commitment. Young people may not be 'right', but only by enlisting their participation through responding initially to their expressed needs and wishes can further intervention be made. And that is why the youth service curriculum, not so much as it stands at present but in terms of the trajectory it is taking, is seriously flawed.

But how are we to hear those voices? The key to successfully interviewing young people must be engagement with them in a role which conveys a sense of 'naive curiosity'. Certainly this writer - who allegedly possesses considerable knowledge and expertise about the youth service from a *professional* point of view - would not conceal or play down such competence, but expresses a desire to grasp issues as they appear from young people's point of view. Conveying an honest and empathetic front seems essential to secure honest and forthright responses. Even if the front is, indeed, a 'front', it needs to be persuasive, for young people are quick to spot, and withdraw co-operation from, individuals (youth workers or researchers) whom they detect are simply doing it 'for themselves'. I have argued elsewhere (Butler and Williamson, 1994) that children and young people respond best to interaction based on Biestek's (1961) time-honoured 'principles of social work': acceptance, confidentiality and a non-judgmental attitude. I have also argued (Williamson, 1996) that commitment and 'passion' will be recognised and respected, and will assist in securing data of greater depth. But that passion needs to be reconciled with receptivity to all kinds of attitudes and perspectives: research work is not the platform to engage in the challenging of racism or homophobia. Rather, qualitative approaches are about unravelling why young people subscribe to the views they hold and about teasing out not only their perspectives but their explanations for them.

Ultimately, like most other respondents in social research, young people in *any* setting are not a captive audience, to have information squeezed out of them. Young people in fact are less likely to possess the 'social graces' which help to guarantee at least some level of co-operation in other social settings frequented by adults. If they don't wish to collaborate, they don't. Thus we have to nurture *their* curiosity in the research, be clear that here is an opportunity to present *their* views, but be honest that their views often are but one part of a much broader 'grid' within which subsequent analysis will be conducted. Their views have special, but not uniquely privileged, status. Without them, the credibility of any analysis will be severely weakened, if not deeply flawed. With their consent and co-operation a more comprehensive picture of policy, provision and practice can be formed, and a more rigorous theoretical formulation composed. And, sometimes, it may be important to assert that if they fail to seize the chance to 'have their say', it will be a missed opportunity: they will be further disempowered and policy will still drive forward, though more blindly as a result.

Indeed, that is exactly how recent policy has been formulated, with scant attention paid to the views of young people. Yet a small qualitative inquiry into the needs, concerns, wants, attitudes and aspirations of young people reveals a modest but coherent set of expectations from users of the youth service, albeit somewhat at odds with prevailing trends. Without taking these into account, the much vaunted principles of youth work recede into a sea of rhetoric which bears little relation to the development of relevant practice.

Through adopting a methodology which takes account of such perspectives, as an integral component of a study of the brave new world of youth work, some salutary lessons can perhaps be learned. If the youth service is true to its intent of serving a broad base of young people, but with a specific focus on more disadvantaged young people, then it needs to retain an eclectic approach which preserves the flexibility to develop considered *reactive* interventions based on negotiation and dialogue with changing constituencies, not simply go for the easy options or become ringfenced by a set of top-down managerial expectations around planning and performance.

There is no doubt that the youth service needs to be moved forward from simply providing 'ping pong and pool'. Young people today are more sophisticated than that. Their *wants* may demand the modern equivalents, such as computer games and music equipment. Their *needs*, in a complex world, are in many ways considerably greater than those which obtained twenty years ago. In some ways, however, they are the same: autonomous social space, adults who are prepared to listen, environments where they can find support and information but choose to use it *as and when they want*. This increasingly is being denied, as those who work with them are expected to produce measurable and specific outcomes. Youth work is, ultimately, an act of faith rather than an act of science, based upon a belief that there is a value in investing in the next generation. It may play only a modest role, and it may occasionally deliver outcomes which are socially undesirable, but it may be the only remaining site within which young people can shape themselves for their entry into adult life.

This chapter has, necessarily, conveyed pessimism about the capacity of the youth service to respond appropriately to the needs of young people in light of ever-increasing political and managerial constraints. A more optimistic reading is that constructive youth work provision can be fitted retrospectively into a 'curriculum framework', providing an opportunity for reflecting on whether or not a spread of relevant provision has been made. But too rigid forward planning of specific interventions and set outcomes is a denial of an opportunity for young people to determine what they want to do - and subsequently plan, implement and evaluate it on their terms (with suitably sensitive professional guidance). It is also, ultimately, a condemnation of a professional service constructed on a person-centred and empowering philosophy.

References

Biestek, F. (1961), *The Casework Relationship*, London: Allen and Unwin.

Blackman, S. (1995), *Youth: Positions and Oppositions*, Aldershot: Avebury.

Brandes, D. and Ginnis, P. (1986), *A Guide to Student-Centred Learning*, Oxford: Basil Blackwell.

Brew, J. Macalister (1946), *Informal Education: Adventures and Reflections*, London: Faber.

Brown, S. (1994), *Whose Challenge? Youth, Crime and Everyday Life in Middlesborough*, Middlesborough: Middlesborough City Challenge Partnership and Middlesborough Safer Cities Project.

Bunt, S. (1990), *Years and Years of Youth*, Croydon: Pro Juventus Press.

Butler, I. and Williamson, H. (1994), *Children Speak: Children, Trauma and Social Work*, London: Longman/NSPCC.

Cashmore, E. and Troyna, B. (eds) (1982), *Black Youth in Crisis*, London: Allen and Unwin.

Cohen, P. (1972), 'Subcultural Conflict and Working Class Community' *Working Papers in Cultural Studies* 2, Centre for Contemporary Cultural Studies, University of Birmingham, Spring, pp 5-51.

Coopers and Lybrand (1994), *Preventative Strategies for Young People at Risk*, London: Prince's Trust

Cunningham, J. and Kotler, M. (1983), *Building Neighborhood Organisations*, Indiana: University of Notre Dame Press

Davies, B. (1986), *Threatening Youth: Towards a National Youth Policy*, Milton Keynes: Open University Press.

Davis, J. (1990), *Youth and The Condition of Britain: Images of Adolescent Conflict*, London: Athlone Press.

Dennison, B. and Kirk, R. (1990), *Do, Review, Learn, Apply: a Simple Guide to Experiential Learning*, Oxford: Blackwell.

Department of Education and Science (1969), *Youth and Community Work in the 70s* (The Milson-Fairbairn Report), London: HMSO.

Department of Education and Science (1982), *Experience and Participation: Report of the Review Group on the Youth Service in England* (The Thompson Report), London: HMSO.

De Wachter, B. and Kristensen, S. (1995), *Promoting the Initiative and Creativity of Young People*, Brussels: European Commission.

Dewdney, A., Grey, C., Minnion, A. and the residents of the Rufford Street Hostel (1994), *Down But Not Out: Young People, Photography and Images of Homelessness*, Stoke-on-Trent: Trentham Books.

Dewey, J. (1963), *Experience and Education*, New York: Macmillan. First published in 1938.

Eggleston, J. (1976), *Adolescence and Community: The Youth Service in Britain*, London: Edward Arnold.

Graef, R. (1992), *Living Dangerously: Young Offenders in their own Words*, London: Harper Collins.

Griffin, C. (1985), *Typical Girls? Young Women from School to the Job Market*, London: Routledge and Kegan Paul.

Hammersley, M. and Atkinson, P. (1995), *Ethnography: Principles in Practice*, London: Tavistock.

Hirst, J. (1994), *Not in Front of the Grown-Ups: a Study of the Social and Sexual Lifestyles of 15 and 16 year olds*, Sheffield Hallam University: PAVIC Publications.

Holden, H. (1972), *Hoxton Cafe Project*, Leicester: Youth Service Information Centre.

Istance, D., Rees, G. and Williamson, H. (1994), *Young People Not in Education, Training or Employment in South Glamorgan*, Cardiff: South Glamorgan Training and Enterprise Council

Jamieson, I., Hunt, D., Richards, B. and Williamson, H. (1988), *The Mini-Enterprise in Schools Project*, London: Department of Trade and Industry.

Jeffs, A. (1979), *Young People and the Youth Service*, London: Routledge and Kegan Paul.

Jeffs, T. and Smith, M. (eds) (1987), *Youth Work*, London: Macmillan.

Jeffs, T. and Smith, M. (eds) (1988), *Welfare and Youth Work Practice*, London: Macmillan.

Jeffs, T. and Smith, M. (1990a), 'Youth Work, Youth Service and the next few years', *Youth and Policy* 31, pp 21-29.

Jeffs, T. and Smith, M. (eds) (1990b), *Young People, Inequality and Youth Work*, London: Macmillan.

Jeffs, T. and Smith, M. (eds) (1990c), *Using Informal Education: an Alternative to Casework, Teaching and Control?*, Buckingham; Open University Press.

Jenkins, R. (1983), *Lads, Citizens and Ordinary Kids: Working-Class Youth Life-styles in Belfast*, London: Routledge and Kegan Paul.

Ministry of Education (1960), *The Youth Service in England and Wales* (The Albemarle Report), London: HMSO.

Mizen, P. (1995), *The State, Young People and Youth Training: In and Against the Training State*, London: Mansell.

National Youth Bureau (1990), *Danger or Opportunity: Towards a Core Curriculum for the Youth Service?*, Leicester: National Youth Bureau.

Rogers, C. (1983), *Freedom to Learn*, Columbus OH: Charles Merrill.

Scanlon, J. (ed.) (1990), *Surviving the Blues: Growing Up in the Thatcher Decade*, London: Virago.

Smith, C., Farrant, M. and Marchant, H. (1972), *The Wincroft Youth Project*, London: Tavistock.

Smith, M. (1988), *Developing Youth Work: Informal Education, Mutual Aid and Popular Practice*, Milton Keynes: Open University Press.

Smith, M. (1994), *Local Education: Community, Conversation, Praxis*, Buckingham: Open University Press.

Springhall, J. (1977), *Youth, Empire and Society: British Youth Movements 1883-1940*, London: Croom Helm.

Welsh Office (1984), *Youth Service Provision in Wales*, Cardiff: Welsh Office/HMSO.

Williamson, H. (1990), 'Curriculum or Collaboration?', *Young People Now*, Vol 1 No 16, p.39.

Williamson, H. (1993), 'Youth Policy in the United Kingdom and the Marginalisation of Young People', *Youth and Policy* 40, Spring, pp 33-48.

Williamson, H. (1995), 'Policy Responses to Youth Unemployment: cultures, careers and consequences for young people', paper presented at Jobs for Young Australians international conference, Adelaide, South Australia.

Williamson, H. (1996), in S. Delamont and K. Carter, *Qualitative Research: The Emotional Dimension*, Aldershot: Avebury.

Williamson, H., Evans, A., Donald, A., Loudon, M. and Howells, M. (1993), *Curriculum in Context: Youth Work in Wales*, University of Wales, Cardiff: School of Education/School of Social and Administrative Studies.

Williamson, H. and Weatherspoon, K. (1985), *Strategies for Intervention*, Cardiff: Ely Community Project.

Willis, P., Bekenn, A., Ellis, T. and Whitt, D. (1988), *The Youth Review: Social Conditions of Young People in Wolverhampton*, Aldershot: Avebury.